REALSCHULE 2005

Abschluss-Prüfungs-
aufgaben mit Lösungen

Englisch
Realschulabschluss
Mecklenburg-Vorpommern
1996–2004

STARK

ISBN: 3-89449-349-6

© 1998 by Stark Verlagsgesellschaft mbH & Co. KG
D-85318 Freising · Postfach 1852 · Tel. (0 81 61) 1790
7. ergänzte Auflage 2004
Nachdruck verboten!

Inhalt

Vorwort
Hinweise zur Abschlussprüfung

Englische Kurzgrammatik

Adverb – Das Umstandswort .... G 1
Auxiliaries and their Substitutes – Hilfszeitwörter und ihre Ersatzformen .... G 5
Comparison of Adjectives – Die Steigerung des Adjektivs .... G 7
Gerund – Das Gerundium .... G 10
If-Clauses – Bedingungssätze .... G 13
Infinitive – Der Infinitiv .... G 14
Participle Construction – Partizipialkonstruktion .... G 16
Passive Voice – Das Passiv .... G 21
Reciprocal Pronoun – Das Fürwort der Gegenseitigkeit .... G 23
Reflexive Pronoun – Das rückbezügliche Fürwort .... G 24
Relative Clauses – Relativsätze .... G 26
Reported Speech – Indirekte Rede .... G 28
Subject and Object Questions – Fragen nach dem Subjekt und dem Objekt ... G 31
Tenses – Die Zeiten .... G 34

Probearbeiten

Probearbeit 1997: Fast Food – Big Money 1
Probearbeit 1998: False Alarm 10
Probearbeit 2000: Listening comprehension .... A 1
  Reading comprehension: Bullying .... A 7

Abschlussprüfungsaufgaben

Abschlussprüfung 1996: Terry 96-1
Abschlussprüfung 1997: Ecstasy 97-1
Abschlussprüfung 1998: Television 98-1
Abschlussprüfung 1999: Fans 99-1
Abschlussprüfung 2000: Listening comprehension 2000-1
  The Truth About Kids Today 2000-7
Abschlussprüfung 2001: Listening comprehension 2001-1
  The Californian Dream 2001-7
Abschlussprüfung 2002: Listening comprehension 2002-1
  Living Clean – Living Cool? 2002-6
Abschlussprüfung 2003: Listening comprehension 2003-1
  Top Teen Twins 2003-6
Abschlussprüfung 2004: Listening comprehension 2004-1
  Eminem 2004-5

Jeweils zu Beginn des neuen Schuljahres erscheinen die neuen
Ausgaben der Abschlussprüfungsaufgaben mit Lösungen.

Autorinnen:

Probearbeiten und Lösungen der Abschluss-Prüfungsaufgaben: Martina Heuser
Kurzgrammatik: Gabriele Achhammer

Vorwort

Dieses Buch richtet sich an euch, liebe Schülerinnen und Schüler, die ihr euch intensiv auf die schriftliche Abschlussprüfung im Fach Englisch vorbereiten wollt.

Wie der Titel schon verdeutlicht, wird euch mit diesem Buch anhand der **Prüfungs- und Probearbeiten** der letzten Jahre die Möglichkeit gegeben, euch gezielt auf den kombinierten Lese- und Hörverstehenstest vorzubereiten. Ihr erhaltet **Hinweise und Tipps** für den Umgang mit den einzelnen Prüfungsabschnitten sowie deren **Lösungen.**

In der Hoffnung, dass dieses Buch und euer ausdauerndes, beharrliches Arbeiten damit, euch Erfolg in der Abschlussprüfung beschert, wünsche ich allen Schülern in Mecklenburg-Vorpommern Zuversicht und Selbstvertrauen.

Wenn ihr euer Hörverstehen noch intensiver üben wollt, könnt ihr dies ideal mit dem Trainingsband für die Realschule: **Englisch Hörverstehen 10. Klasse** (Stark Verlag Titel-Nr. 91457). Er enthält 20 unterhaltsame und informative Texte – von Muttersprachlern auf CD gesprochen – und abwechslungsreiche Aufgaben, die das Hörverstehen verbessern. Die prüfungsrelevanten Übungstypen sind enthalten.

Martina Heuser

Hinweise zur Abschlussprüfung

1 Allgemeine Anmerkungen

Gemäß der veränderten Verordnung über die Durchführung der Abschlussprüfung besteht die schriftliche Prüfung für das **Fach Englisch aus einem kombinierten Lese- und Hörverstehenstest.**

2 Aufbau des kombinierten Lese- und Hörverstehenstests

Der **Hörverstehenstext** umfasst **3 Teilaufgaben** (die unter **Punkt 3.1** näher erläutert werden). Der **Leseverstehensteil** der Prüfungsarbeit besteht aus **5 Abschnitten** (die unter **Punkt 3.2** näher erklärt werden):
- Comprehension,
- Language,
- Grammar,
- Using the language in different contexts,
- Comment/Giving Opinion.

3 Hinweise zu den einzelnen Teilaufgaben

3.1 Hörverstehenstest

Dein Hörverstehen wird durch folgende **Aufgabenformen** überprüft:
- Ankreuzen der richtigen Antwort (tick, make a cross)
- Verbinden von Sätzen (connect, match)
- Fehlerhafte Informationen unter- oder wegstreichen (underline errors)
- Fehler korrigieren (correct errors)
- Vervollständigen von Sätzen (complete, fill in gaps)
- Sätze in die richtige Reihenfolge bringen (put in the correct order)

3.2. Leseverstehenstest

Die **Arbeitszeit** für den Leseverstehenstest beträgt **160 Minuten** und beginnt mit dem Lesen des Textes. Diesem können beispielsweise ein **Zeitungsartikel**, ein **Dialog**, ein **Brief** oder eine **Rede** zugrunde liegen. Es folgen Erläuterungen zu den Aufgabenformen.

3.2.1 Comprehension

Dieser Teil umfasst zwei Aufgaben, die **dein Textverständnis** überprüfen. *Matching exercise* bedeutet, du musst **bestimmte Satzhälften** einander richtig **zuordnen**. In der 2. Teilaufgabe hast du zu **entscheiden**, ob eine Feststellung **richtig** oder **falsch** *(true/false)* ist.

3.2.2 Language

In diesem Teil sollst du nachweisen, inwieweit du wichtige **Wörter** oder **ihre Synonyme** sowie **Strukturen aus dem Text** verstanden hast und in der Lage bist, den **Lückentext** *(gap text)* richtig zu **vervollständigen**.

3.2.3 Grammar

Im dritten Teil werden deine Kenntnisse zu verschiedenen **grammatischen Phänomenen** überprüft. Falls du mit der richtigen Verwendung der Grammatik noch Schwierigkeiten hast, so kann dir die diesem Leitfaden nachgestellte Kurz-Grammatik eine Hilfe sein.

3.2.4 Using the language in different contexts

In diesem Teil sollst du die bisher im **Text** aufgetauchten **Vokabeln** und Ideen **in einem anderen Zusammenhang verwenden**. So musst du z. B. einen **Lückendialog** *(defective dialogue)* vervollständigen bzw. **Fragen** zu vorgegebenen **Antworten** (oder umgekehrt) finden.

3.2.5 Comment

In dieser letzten Teilaufgabe hast du einen **in sich geschlossenen Text** zu **einem oder zwei Aspekten des Themas mit persönlicher Stellungnahme und Begründungen** zu schreiben. Für die Bewältigung der Aufgaben 3.2.4 und 3.2.5 können dir folgende Wörter und Wendungen helfen.

- **Argumentation**

  In my opinion, ... Meiner Meinung nach ...
  To my mind, ... Meiner Auffassung nach ...
  I (don't) think that ... Ich denke (nicht), dass ...
  I (don't) believe that ... Ich glaube (nicht), dass ...
  I would (not) say that ... Ich würde (nicht) sagen, dass ...
  I can (not) agree with ... Ich kann (nicht) dem ... zustimmen ...
  I am convinced that ... Ich bin überzeugt, dass ...
  I must contradict ... Ich muss widersprechen ...
  One reason is that ... Ein Grund ist, dass ...
  This statement is contradictory because ... Diese Aussage ist widersprüchlich, weil ...

- **Conclusion**

  As a result ... Als Ergebnis ...
  I have come to the conclusion ... Ich bin zu der Schlussfolgerung gelangt ...
  To sum up ... Zusammenfassend ...

- **Verbindungswörter**

Reihenfolge/ Aufzählung/Zeit:	*First(ly)...*	Zuerst, erstens...
	Second(ly)...	Zweitens...
	Furthermore...	Weiterhin...
	Then...	Dann...
	Finally,...	Schließlich...
	While...	Während...
	Since...	Seit...
Begründung:	*As...*	Da...
	Because of...	Wegen...
	Because...	Weil...
	Therefore...	Deswegen...
	That's why...	Deshalb...
Gegensatz:	*But...*	Aber/Sondern...
	In contrast to...	Im Gegensatz zu...
Bedingung:	*If...*	Wenn/Falls...
	Whether...	Ob...
	Although...	Obwohl...
	However...	Trotzdem/Jedoch...
Beispiel:	*For example...*	Zum Beispiel...
	For instance...	Zum Beispiel...

Wie du siehst, ist der **Leseverstehenstest** so angelegt, dass du von **einfachen Aufgabenformen** (Ankreuzen der richtigen Antwort, Auswahl der passenden Wörter) zu **schwierigen Aufgaben** (Schreiben von Sätzen und schließlich eines zusammenhängendes Textes) geführt wirst.

4 Hinweise zur Durchführung der Prüfung und zum Vorgehen

Vor der Durchführung des *Hörverstehenstests* erhältst du die **Aufgabenblätter**, gestempeltes Notizpapier sowie **ein englisch-deutsches Wörterbuch**. Euer Fachlehrer stimmt euch kurz in englischer Sprache auf die Thematik ein. Danach werden die **3 Texte** vom Lehrer zunächst **einmal** vorgelesen, wobei ihr **vor jedem Vorlesen** die Möglichkeit habt, euch mit den **Aufgabenstellungen** vertraut zu machen. Der Lehrer darf auch **Erläuterungen** zu den Aufgaben geben. Während des zweiten Vorlesens bearbeitet ihr das Aufgabenblatt und könnt euch gegebenenfalls auch Notizen machen. Die reine Prüfungszeit beträgt **20 Minuten**.

Vor dem *Leseverstehenstest* erhältst du das **gesamte Testmaterial** (Text und Aufgaben). **Das englisch-deutsche Wörterbuch** steht dir selbstverständlich auch wieder zur Verfügung. **Lies zuerst den Text und die Aufgabenstellungen gründlich durch!** Dafür stehen dir **15 Minuten** zur Verfügung. **Vokabelerklärungen** zum Text kannst du vom Lehrer **nicht** erwarten. Aber Wörter, die sich auf die **Aufgabenstellungen** beziehen, dürfen vom Lehrer erläutert werden. Wie bereits erwähnt, hast du **160 Minuten** Zeit für die Bearbeitung des Leseverstehenstests.
Hier noch einige Begriffe, die dir das Verständnis der **Aufgabenstellungen** erleichtern:

- **Allgemeine Aufgabenstellung**
according to	entsprechend
blank	Textlücke
in brackets	in Klammern
to choose	auswählen
comes close in meaning to	ist ähnlich in der Bedeutung wie
to combine	kombinieren, verbinden
context	Gesamtzusammenhang
to copy	wörtlich abschreiben
corresponding to	entsprechend
to correct/correct	verbessern/richtig
different from	verschieden von, anders als
to explain/explanation	erklären/Erklärung
false	falsch, unwahr
to fill in	(in) Lücken einsetzen/ausfüllen
gap	Lücke
item	Stichwort, neuer Gedanke, Gesichtspunkt, (Tagesordnungs-)Punkt
to join sentences	Sätze verbinden
to leave out	auslassen
to mean/meaning	bedeuten/Bedeutung
missing word	fehlendes Wort
negative/to make negative	negativ, verneint/verneinen
opinion	Meinung
paragraph	Textabschnitt
to reread/write	nochmals lesen/schreiben
right	richtig
reason	Grund, Begründung
result, effect	Ergebnis, Wirkung
similar	ähnlich
situation	Situation
space	Raum: zur Verfügung stehender Platz
suitable, proper	passend
to think	meinen, glauben
true	wahr
wrong	falsch

- **Wortschatzaufgaben**
word formation	Wortbildung
word family	Wortfamilie
prefix/suffix	Vor-/Nachsilbe
synonym/opposite	Wort möglichst ähnlicher/entgegengesetzter Bedeutung
generic term	allgemeiner Begriff, Oberbegriff

Quellenverzeichnis
Schriftliche Realabschlussprüfung in der 1. Fremdsprache Mecklenburg-Vorpommern, Handreichungen für Schüler, 1996

Adverb – Das Umstandswort

Adverbien dienen zur näheren Bestimmung von **Verben, Adjektiven** und **anderen Adverbien**. Nach einem Adverb fragt man immer mit **"wie"**. Bevor Du also ein Adverb bildest, mußt Du den englischen Satz analysieren!

Bildung	Anhängen von -**ly** an das **Adjektiv**.	slow – slow**ly**
	y → i	happ**y** – happ**ily**
		Ausnahme: shy**ly**
	auf einen Mitlaut folgendes le → ly	simp**le** – simp**ly**
	ic → ically	automat**ic** – automat**ically**
		Ausnahme: pub**licly**
	stummes -e bleibt	extrem**e** – extrem**ely**
		Ausnahmen: fully, wholly, truly

1. Aufgaben des Adverbs

a) Nähere Bestimmung eines Vollverbs

He	**drives**	slowly.
Wie	**fährt** er?	langsam

Beachte: Bildet das Adjektiv mit einem Hilfsverb (Formen von to be) das Prädikat, so muß es als Adjektiv erhalten bleiben.

He is slow.
 └─┬─┘
 Prädikat

b) Nähere Bestimmung eines Adjektivs

	He is	**extremely**	**slow.**
Wie **langsam**	ist er?	äußerst	langsam

c) Nähere Bestimmung eines anderen Adverbs

He drives	**extremely**	slow**ly.**
Wie fährt er?		langsam
Wie **langsam** fährt er?	äußerst	(langsam)

G 1

Beachte die Stellung, wenn zwei Adverbien im Satz stehen: Dasjenige Adverb (1), das ein anderes Adverb (2) bestimmt, muß vor diesem Adverb, das es bestimmt, stehen.

       1   2
He drives extremely slowly.   (1) bestimmt (2)

2. Attributiver Gebrauch des Adjektivs

Beachte: Du darfst aus einem Adjektiv, das einem Substantiv beigefügt ist, kein Adverb bilden!
He is a **slow** driver.

3. Besonderheiten in der Bildung von Adverbien

a) Endet das Adjektiv bereits auf -ly, so muß das Adverb gebildet werden mit einer Umschreibung von **"in a ... way"**, **"in a ... manner"**.
She asked me **in a friendly way/manner**.

b) Nach bestimmten Verben (**Zustandsverben**, die keine Handlung, sondern einen Zustand beschreiben) darf das Adjektiv **nicht** zum **Adverb** werden, obwohl es das Verb näher bestimmt.
It sounds **good**.

Weitere Zustandsverben:	to become	werden
	to feel	sich fühlen
	to get	werden
	to keep	bleiben, halten
	to look	aussehen
	to remain	bleiben
	to seem	scheinen
	to smell	riechen
	to sound	klingen
	to stay	bleiben, halten
	to taste	schmecken

c) Manche Adverbien haben die **gleiche Form wie Adjektive**, da ansonsten eine **Bedeutungsveränderung** eintritt.
I work **hard**.   Ich arbeite **schwer**.
I **hardly** work.   Ich arbeite **kaum**.

unveränderte Adverbien:	early	früh
	far	weit
	fast	schnell
	hard	schwer
	high	hoch
	late	spät
	long	lang
	near	nahe
Bedeutungsveränderung:	hardly	kaum
	highly	hoch, sehr (abstrakt)
	lately	in letzter Zeit
	nearly	beinahe, fast

d) good → well

She rides very **well**.
Beachte: to be well = gesund sein
I didn't go to work because I wasn't **well** yesterday.

4. Die Steigerung des Adverbs

a) Adverbien auf -ly werden mit **"more"** und **"most"** bzw. mit **"less"** (weniger) **"least"** (am wenigsten) gesteigert.

He drives **more** (less) slowly than she does.
He drives **most** (least) slow**ly**.

b) Adverbien mit der gleichen Form wie Adjektive (siehe 3 c) werden mit **-er, -est** gesteigert.

fast – faster – fastest;
high – higher – highest;
early – earlier – earliest

He works hard**er** than Tony.
Pupils study hard**est** before a test.

c) unregelmäßige Formen:

well – better   – best
badly – worse   – worst
far   – farther/further – farthest/furthest

5. Die Stellung des Adverbs

a) Das **Adverb der Art und Weise** steht normalerweise am **Satzende**; es darf nie zwischen Verb und direktem Objekt stehen!
He waited **patiently**.

b) **Gradadverbien** stehen **vor** dem Wort, das sie näher bestimmen; zu den Gradadverbien zählen "extremely, extraordinarily, absolutely, fairly, pretty, rather, quite, very, terribly, especially, really, particularly, much, a bit" usw.
He drives **extremely** carefully.

c) **Häufigkeitsadverbien** wie "often, seldom, rarely, always, never, occasionally, frequently" stehen
- **vor** dem gebeugten **Vollverb**
He **always** reads the newspaper in the morning.
- **nach** dem **1. Hilfs- oder Modalverb** bei zusammengesetzten Zeiten
He has **never** visited the British Museum.
- **nach "to be"**
We are **already** at home.

d) **Adverbien bzw. adverbiale Bestimmungen der Zeit und des Ortes** sowie "in fact, unfortunately, luckily, of course, perhaps, actually" gehören entweder an den **Satzanfang** oder an das **Satzende**.

Three minutes later the boy arrived.
The boy arrived **three minutes later**.

Kurzgrammatik

Auxiliaries and their Substitutes – Hilfszeitwörter und ihre Ersatzformen

Es gibt zwei Arten von Hilfszeitwörtern
- **primäre** oder **vollständige** Hilfszeitwörter (complete auxiliaries): to be
to have
to do
Mit den vollständigen Hilfszeitwörtern bildet man Fragen, Verneinungen, Kurzantworten und Zeiten.
- **modale** Hilfszeitwörter (modal auxiliaries): Sie drücken aus, daß etwas geschehen kann, muß, darf, soll, könnte etc. Sie werden in Verbindung mit einem Vollverb verwendet, haben aber in der 3. Person Singular kein -s. Sie können auch nicht alle Zeiten bilden und brauchen deshalb **bestimmte Ersatzformen,** deren wichtigste Du Dir einprägen mußt.

1. must

must = to have to = müssen   I **don't** have to come.
Do I have to come?

Die Ersatzform gilt hier als Vollverb und muß deshalb in Frage und Verneinung umschrieben werden.

Simple Present:	I have to come.	I don't have to come.
Simple Past:	I had to come.	I didn't have to come.
Present Perfect:	I have had to come.	I haven't had to come.
Past Perfect:	I had had to come.	I hadn't had to come.
Future I:	I will have to come.	I won't have to come.
Future II:	I will have had to come.	I won't have had to come.
Beachte die Bedeutungsveränderung:		
must not (mustn't)	= not to be allowed to	= nicht **dürfen**

2. can

can = to be able to = können, fähig sein

Simple Present:	I am (not) able to play the piano.
Simple Past:	I was (not) able to play ...
Present Perfect:	I have (not) been able to play ...
Past Perfect:	I had (not) been able to play ...
Future I:	I will (not) be able to play ...
Future II:	I will (not) have been able to play ...

G 5

3. may

may = to be allowed to = dürfen

> He ist (not) allowed to come.

4. shall/should/ought to

shall/should/ought to = to be supposed to = sollen
　　　　　　　　　　　to be expected to
　　　　　　　　　　　to be to

> He **is (not) supposed** to win the match.
> He **is expected to** win ...
> He **is to** ask the manager.

5. need

need　　= to have to　　　= brauchen, müssen
needn't = not to have to　= nicht brauchen, nicht müssen

> You **needn't** come. = You **don't have to** come.

Comparison of Adjectives – Die Steigerung des Adjektivs

1. **Die Steigerung des Adjektivs auf -er, est**

   a) **Einsilbige Adjektive** werden im Komparativ (1. Steigerungsstufe) auf **-er**, im Superlativ (2. Steigerungsstufe) auf **-est** gesteigert.

Grundform:	cheap	billig
Komparativ:	cheap**er**	billig**er**
Superlativ:	cheap**est**	am billig**sten**

   b) **Zweisilbige Adjektive**, die auf **-er, -le, -y, -ow** enden, bilden normalerweise die Steigerung ebenfalls mit **-er, -est**.

clev**er**	clever**er**	clever**est**	klug	klüger	am klügsten
simp**le**	simp**ler**	simp**lest**	einfach	einfacher	am einfachsten
ug**ly**	ug**lier**	ug**liest**	häßlich	häßlicher	am häßlichsten
narr**ow**	narrow**er**	narrow**est**	eng	enger	am engsten

   c) **Besonderheiten in der Schreibung**

stummes **-e** am Wortende fällt weg	large – larg**er** – larg**est** fine – fin**er** – fin**est**
Konsonant (Mitlaut) am Wortende wird nach einem kurzen, betonten Vokal (Selbstlaut a, e, i, o, u) verdoppelt	hot – hot**ter** – hot**test** glad – glad**der** – glad**dest**
y → i nach einem Konsonanten *Beachte:* y bleibt nach Vokalen erhalten	happy – happ**ier** – happ**iest** sunny – sunn**ier** – sunn**iest** gay – gay**er** – gay**est**

2. **Die Steigerung des Adjektivs mit more, most**

   a) **Zweisilbige Adjektive**, bei denen Regel 1 b nicht in Kraft tritt, bilden den Komparativ mit **more** und den Superlativ mit **most**.

Grundform:	famous	berühmt
Komparativ:	**more** famous	berühmter
Superlativ:	**most** famous	am berühmtesten

G 7

Kurzgrammatik

b) **Drei- und mehrsilbige Adjektive** werden ebenfalls mit **more, most** gesteigert.

difficult	–	**more** difficult	–	**most** difficult
schwierig	–	schwieriger	–	am schwierigsten
comfortable	–	**more** comfortable	–	**most** comfortable
bequem	–	bequemer	–	am bequemsten

3. Unregelmäßige Steigerungsformen

good – better – best	gut – besser – am besten
bad – worse – worst ill – worse – worst	schlecht – schlechter – am schlechtesten krank – kränker – am kränksten
much – more – most many – more – most	viel – mehr – am meisten viele – mehr – am meisten
little – less – least	wenig – weniger – am wenigsten
far – farther – farthest far – further – furthest	weit – weiter – am weitesten weit – weiter – am weitesten
near – nearer – nearest near – nearer – next	nah – näher – am nächsten nah – näher – am nächsten
old – older – oldest old – elder – eldest	alt – älter – am ältesten alt – älter – am ältesten

Beachte die Bedeutungsunterschiede:

less money	weniger Geld	"less" in Verbindung mit **abstrakten** Substantiven
fewer friends	weniger Freunde	"fewer" in Verbindung mit **zählbaren** Begriffen, die in die Mehrzahl gesetzt werden können
farther south	weiter südlich	"farther" nur in bezug auf die **räumliche** Entfernung
further information **further** south	weitere Information weiter südlich	"further" sowohl im **übertragenen** Sinn mit abstrakten Substantiven als auch im **räumlichen** Sinn

the **nearest** pub	das nächste Pub	"nearest" gibt die **räumliche** Entfernung an
the **next** train leaves	der nächste Zug fährt ab	"next" bezeichnet die **Reihenfolge**
my **elder** brother	mein älterer Bruder	"elder" hauptsächlich bei **Verwandtschaftsbezeichnungen**
he is **older** than	er ist älter als	"older" kann **jederzeit** auch bei Verwandtschaftsbezeichnungen verwendet werden
your **last** chance the **latest** fashion	deine **letzte** Chance die **neueste** Mode	

4. Gebrauch der Steigerungsformen im Satz

a) **Grundform**
 (Vergleich von gleichwertigen Dingen)

Our house is **as** cheap **as** yours.
Unser Haus ist **so** billig **wie** eueres.
Our house is not **as** beautiful **as** yours.

b) **Komparativ**
 Signalwort "than" = "als"

Our house is bigg**er than** yours.
Unser Haus ist größ**er als** eueres.
Our house is **more** beautiful **than** yours.
Our house is **less** beautiful **than** yours.
... ist **weniger** schön **als** ...

c) **Superlativ**
 Signalwort "the" = "am"

Our house is **the** cheap**est** house (of all).
Unser Haus ist **das** billig**ste** von allen.
Our house is **the most** beautiful of all.
Our house is **the least** beautiful of all.
... ist das **am wenigsten** schöne ...

5. Spezielle Fälle

a) "**the** ... **the**" = "je ... desto"

The longer you wait **the** better.
Je länger du wartest, desto besser.

b) "... **-er** and **-er**",
 "... **more** and **more**" =
 "**immer** ... **-er**" (zusätzliche Steigerung)

It's getting cold**er** and cold**er**.
Es wird **immer** kälter.
It became **more and more** interesting.
Es wurde **immer** interessant**er**.

c) "**most**" = "**very**" = "äußerst, sehr, höchst"

It's a **most** (= very) interesting book.
Es ist ein **höchst** interessantes Buch.

d) Wiederholung des Hilfszeitwortes am Ende des Satzes

Tony is taller than Tom (**is**).
Tony ist größer als Tom.
The book is more exciting than the film (**is**).
Das Buch ist aufregender als der Film.

Kurzgrammatik

Gerund – Das Gerundium

Bildung	-ing an die Grundform des Verbs
	talk – talking — Normalfall
	write – writing — *Sonderfall:* stummes -e entfällt
	run – running — *Sonderfall:* Verdoppelung des Endkonsonanten

Verwendung	Es werden nur die üblichen Ausdrücke angeführt; ergänze evtl. anhand Deines Englischbuches.

1. **Gerundium als Substantiv (als Subjekt des Satzes)**
   Swimming is fun. (Schwimmen macht Spaß.)

2. **Gerundium nach bestimmten Verben (als Objekt des Satzes)**
   She can't **give up** smoking.

to admit	zugeben	to keep	weitermachen
to avoid	vermeiden	to mention	erwähnen
to deny	leugnen	to mind	etw. ausmachen
to dislike	nicht mögen	not to mind	nichts dagegen haben
to enjoy	genießen	to miss	verpassen
to feel like	Lust haben zu	to practise	üben
to finish	beenden	to remember	erinnern
to forget	vergessen	to risk	(es) wagen, riskieren
to give up	aufgeben	to stop	aufhören
to go/carry on	weitermachen	to suggest	vorschlagen
to imagine	sich (etw.) vorstellen	to try	probieren

3. **Gerundium nach Verb + Präposition**
   I must **apologize for** being late.

to agree with	einverstanden sein	to consist of	bestehen aus
to apologize for	sich entschuldigen für	to dream of/about	träumen von
to believe in	glauben an	to feel like	Lust haben auf
to blame for	tadeln wegen	to insist on	bestehen auf
to complain about	sich beschweren über	to look forward to	sich freuen auf

object to	dagegen sein	to talk about	reden über
to prevent from	hindern an	to thank for	danken für
to protect from	schützen vor	to think of	denken an
to rely on	sich verlassen auf	to worry about	sich Sorgen
to succeed in	gelingen, Erfolg haben		machen über

4. Gerundium nach Adjektiv + Präposition

I am **fond of** travel**ling**.

afraid of	(sich) fürchten	sorry about/for	(jdm.) leid tun, daß
famous for	berühmt wegen	tired of/sick of	es satt haben, es leid sein
fond of	mögen	used for	benützt werden für
good at/bad at	gut/schlecht in	used to	gewohnt
interested in	interessiert an	worried about	besorgt wegen
proud of	stolz auf		

Beachte den Bedeutungsunterschied:
I **am used** to work**ing** hard.   Ich **bin es gewohnt,** schwer zu arbeiten.
I **used to work** hard.   **Früher** arbeitete ich schwer.

5. Gerundium nach einem Substantiv

a) nach Substantiv

Young people often have **trouble** get**ting** a job.

trouble/problem	Schwierigkeiten, Problem(e)
difficulty	Schwierigkeiten
fun	Spaß

b) nach Substantiv + Präposition

She has **difficulty (in)** do**ing** the test.

advantage of	Vorteil von	interest in	Interesse an
chance of	(günstige) Gelegenheit	pleasure in	Freude an
in danger of	in Gefahr	possibility of	Möglichkeit zu
difficulty (in)	Schwierigkeit(en) mit	reason for	Grund für
hope of	Hoffnung zu/auf	trouble in	Schwierigkeiten mit
idea of	Vorstellung, Einfall (zu)	way of	Art und Weise/Weg zu

Kurzgrammatik

6. Gerundium nach Präpositionen

Instead of wait**ing** for me he ran away.

after	nach	in spite of	trotz(dem)
apart from	abgesehen von, außer	instead of	anstatt, statt
before	vor	on	gleich nach(dem)
by	dadurch daß, indem	without	ohne, ohne zu
in	indem		

7. Gerundium nach bestimmten Ausdrücken

This book is **worth** buy**ing**.
It's **no use** ask**ing**.

worth	wert
no use	es hat keinen Sinn
what about/how about	wie wär's mit ...

8. Die Übersetzung des Gerundiums

Es ist oft nicht leicht, das "gerund" ins Deutsche zu übersetzen. Dazu bieten sich verschiedene Möglichkeiten an.

a) **Substantivierung des Verbs:** He can't **give up smoking**.
Er kann **das Rauchen** nicht aufgeben.

b) **Eine Infinitivkonstruktion:** He was **interested in running** a farm.
Er war **daran** interessiert, eine Farm **zu betreiben**.

c) **Ein abhängiger Nebensatz:** She overcame her nervousness **by eating** chocolate.
Sie überwand ihre Nervosität, **indem sie (dadurch, daß sie)** Schokolade aß.
These are the new books **worth buying**.
Dies sind die neuen Bücher, **die es wert sind,** gekauft zu werden.

If-Clauses – Bedingungssätze

Bedingungssätze sind Nebensätze, die ausdrücken, daß unter einer bestimmten Bedingung etwas geschehen kann. Sie werden im Deutschen mit "wenn" oder "falls" eingeleitet, im Englischen mit "if". Der if-Satz kann vor oder nach dem Hauptsatz stehen; falls er vor dem Hauptsatz steht, so muß er durch ein Komma abgetrennt werden.

if-clause (Nebensatz)	main clause (Hauptsatz)
If it rains,	I will take my umbrella.
oder	
main clause (Hauptsatz)	if-clause (Nebensatz)
I will take my umbrella	if it rains.

Man unterscheidet drei Grundarten von if-Sätzen:

1. Tpy 1

Wir verwenden Typ 1, wenn wir über eine Handlung sprechen, die unter einer bestimmten Bedingung in der **Zukunft** geschehen kann. Die **Erfüllung** dieser Bedingung ist **wahrscheinlich**. Dann steht im **if-Satz** das **simple present** und im **Hauptsatz** das **future I**.

If it rains,	I **will** take my umbrella.
Wenn es regnet,	nehme ich meinen Regenschirm.

2. Typ 2

Wir verwenden Typ 2, wenn wir über eine Handlung sprechen, die unter einer bestimmten Bedingung in der **Zukunft** eintreten könnte, aber eher **unwahrscheinlich** ist. Dann steht im **if-Satz** das **simple past** und im **Hauptsatz** das **conditional I**.

If it rain**ed**,	I **would** take my umbrella.
Wenn es regnete/regnen würde,	würde ich meinen Regenschirm nehmen.

3. Typ 3

Wir verwenden Typ 3, wenn wir über eine Bedingung in der **Vergangenheit** sprechen, die **nicht mehr erfüllbar** ist. Dann steht im **if-Satz** das **past perfect** und im **Hauptsatz** das **conditional II**.

If it **had rained**,	I **would have taken** my umbrella.
Wenn es geregnet hätte,	hätte ich meinen Regenschirm genommen.

Infinitive – Der Infinitiv

1. Der Infinitiv

Der Infinitiv mit "to" steht nach

a) bestimmten Verben: She **managed to get** a job.

can afford	sich leisten können	to manage	zustande bringen
to agree	zustimmen	to offer	anbieten
to arrange	vereinbaren	to plan	planen
to attempt	versuchen	to promise	versprechen
to choose	wählen	to refuse	verweigern
to decide	entscheiden	to remember	daran denken
to expect	erwarten	to seem	scheinen
to fail	versagen	to try	versuchen
to forget	vergessen	to want	wollen
to hope	hoffen	would like/love	gern möchten
to learn	lernen		

b) Substantiven: It's a good **idea to visit** London.

c) Adjektiven: It's **easy to find** the way to the post office.

d) Fragewörtern: I don't know **what to do**.

what	where	which	how	who	when	why

2. Objekt + Infinitiv

Im Deutschen wird diese Objekt + Infinitiv-Konstruktion mit einem "daß"-Satz wiedergegeben:

Mary wants **him** **to come**.   Mary will, **daß** er kommt.
    ↓ ↓
   Objekt Infinitiv

Diese Objekt + Infinitiv-Konstruktion steht nach

a) folgenden Verben: I persuaded her to come.

to advise	raten	to invite	einladen
to allow	erlauben	to persuade	überreden, -zeugen
to ask	bitten	to remind	daran erinnern
to cause	verursachen	to teach	lehren
to enable	befähigen	to tell	befehlen
to encourage	ermutigen	to want	wollen
to expect	erwarten	to warn	warnen
to force	zwingen	would like/love	gerne mögen
to get	veranlassen	would prefer	vorziehen
to help	helfen		

b) Verb + Präposition: I'm still **waiting for him to answer** my letter.

to arrange for	vereinbaren, abmachen	to rely on	sich verlassen auf
to count on	rechnen mit	to wait for	warten auf

c) Adjektiv + Präposition: It was **kind of her to wait.**
It's **important for you to learn.**

clever of	klug	nice of	nett
dangerous for	gefährlich	normal for	normal
easy/difficult for	leicht/schwierig	possible for	möglich
good of	liebenswürdig	silly of	dumm
important for	wichtig	tactful of	taktvoll
kind of	freundlich	useful for	nützlich
necessary for	notwendig	usual/unusual for	gewöhnlich/ungewöhnlich

d) Substantiv + Präposition: It's a good **opportunity for me to see** her.

idea for	Idee	chance for/opportunity for	Gelegenheit
mistake for	Fehler	time for	Zeit

e) einem Adjektiv, das durch "too" oder "enough" näher bestimmt wird.

The weather is **too bad for the plane to take off.**
Is the letter **big enough for you to see?**

Participle Construction – Partizipialkonstruktion

Es gibt zwei Arten von Partizipien
- Present Participle (Mittelwort der Gegenwart/Partizip Präsens)
- Past Participle (Mittelwort der Vergangenheit/Partizip Perfekt)

1. Present Participle = Mittelwort der Gegenwart

Bildung			
	-ing an die Grundform des Verbs	talk	– talking
	stummes -e fällt weg	write	– writing
	Mitlaut nach kurzem, betontem Vokal wird verdoppelt	cut	– cutting,
		stop	– stopping,
		travel	– travelling,
		occur	– occurring

2. Past Participle = Mittelwort der Vergangenheit

a) regelmäßige Verben

Bildung			
	-ed an die Grundform des Verbs	talk	– talked
	y → i	carry	– carried
		Ausnahme:	played
	stummes -e fällt weg	live	– lived
	Mitlaut am Wortende wird verdoppelt	stop	– stopped,
		travel	– travelled,
		prefer	– preferred

b) unregelmäßige Verben
   (mußt du auswendig lernen)

Bildung	die dritte Form	write – wrote – **written**

Das Partizip hat die Aufgabe,
- einen Nebensatz zu verkürzen oder
- Hauptsätze mit demselben Subjekt zu verbinden.

3. Verkürzung von Nebensätzen durch ein Partizip

As he wanted to win he practised a lot.
Wanting to win he practised a lot.

Gehe dabei in der angegebenen Reihenfolge vor!

a) **Bestimme** als erstes Hauptsatz (HS) und Nebensatz (NS), denn Du darfst nur den Nebensatz verkürzen! **Der Hauptsatz bleibt immer unverändert!**
Wir erkennen einen NS an:

Konjunktion des Grundes	as, because, since
Konjunktion der Zeit	when, while, after, before
Relativpronomen	who (für Personen), which (für Dinge)

b) Als nächstes prüfst Du, um welche **Art des Nebensatzes** es sich handelt; bei Partizipialverkürzungen kommen nur folgende Nebensätze in Frage:

Nebensatz des Grundes:	die Bindewörter "as, because, since" fallen weg
Nebensatz der Zeit:	die Bindewörter "when, while, before" bleiben erhalten, "after" kann wegfallen
Relativsatz:	die Relativpronomen "who" bzw. "which" fallen weg

	NS		HS	HS		NS
As	he was	ill	he couldn't come.	I saw a man	who	cleaned his car.
–	**Being**	ill	he couldn't come.	I saw a man		cleaning his car.

c) Dann überlegst Du Dir, ob HS und NS dasselbe **Subjekt** haben.

• Haben HS und NS **dasselbe Subjekt**, so fällt das Subjekt im NS weg:

	S_1			S_2		
As	Tony	was	ill	he	couldn't come.	$S_1 = S_2$
–	–	Being	ill	he	couldn't come.	

• Haben HS und NS **verschiedene Subjekte**, so müssen beide genannt werden. Jedoch wird in den meisten Fällen die Partizipialkonstruktion vermieden.

S_1 S_2
The holidays coming to an end, **the pupils** went back to school. $S_1 \neq S_2$

d) Schließlich mußt Du noch die **Zeit im NS** beachten.

Present Tense:	he arrives	Present Perfect:	he has arrived
Past Tense:	he arrived	Past Perfect:	he had arrived
↓	↓	↓	↓ ↓
Present Participle:	arriving	**Perfect Participle:**	having arrived

When he	arrives		he takes off his coat.
	↓		
When –	arriving		he takes off his coat.

After he	had	arrived	he took off his coat.
	↓		
(After) –	having	arrived	he took off his coat.

e) Ist der **NS verneint**, so mußt Du "not" vor das Partizip setzen. Die Umschreibung mit "do, does, did" fällt weg.

As he	did	not	practise	he failed in the examination.
– –	–	Not	practising	he failed in the examination.

4. Verbindung von Hauptsätzen durch ein Partizip

Dies ist nur möglich, wenn die Hauptsätze **dasselbe Subjekt** haben. Meistens sind sie durch "and" verbunden. Beachte folgende Punkte:

- Ein Hauptsatz, meistens der erste, bleibt unverändert erhalten.
- "and" als Verbindung der Hauptsätze fällt weg.
- Subjekt 2 fällt ebenfalls weg, da es mit Subjekt 1 übereinstimmt.
- Aus dem Verb des zu verkürzenden Hauptsatzes wird das Partizip.

S_1		S_2			
He sat in his chair	and	he	smoked	a pipe.	$S_1 = S_2$
He sat in his chair	–	–	smoking	a pipe.	

5. Auflösung einer Partizipialkonstruktion in einen Nebensatz

a) Als erstes suchst Du das Partizip im Satz und unterstreichst es. Dann überlegst Du, um welche **Art von Nebensatz** es sich dabei handeln kann.

- Handelt es sich um einen **NS der Zeit**, so mußt Du, falls kein Bindewort vorhanden ist, den Nebensatz mit einem passenden Bindewort einleiten, wie z. B. mit "when, while, after, before."

–	–	Having	come home we drank tea.
After	we	had	come home we drank tea.

- **Nebensätze des Grundes** mußt Du mit "as, because, since" einleiten.

–	–	Talking	to her	he missed the bus.
As	(because)	he	talked	to her	he missed the bus.

- **Relativsätze** müssen mit dem Relativpronomen "who" oder "which" beginnen. Du kannst einen verkürzten Nebensatz erkennen:

an einem dem Partizip direkt vorausgehenden Substantiv

I watched a **man**	–	taking	a photo of his mother.
I watched a **man**	who	took	a photo of his mother.

wenn kein present participle, sondern nur ein past participle im Satz steht (Auflösung durch einen Passivsatz/Signalwort "by")

He saw a **book**	–		written **by** his friend.
He saw a **book**	which	was	written **by** his friend.

b) Als nächstes suchst Du das **Subjekt** im HS und im NS. Ist im verkürzten NS **kein Subjekt** vorhanden, so übernimmst Du das Subjekt des Hauptsatzes.

When	–	preparing	supper	I	always listen to the radio.
When	I	prepare	supper	I	always listen to the radio.

c) Schließlich überlegst Du Dir die **Zeit**, in der der Nebensatz stehen soll. Dabei orientierst Du Dich an der Zeit des Hauptsatzes.

When	visiting	the Tower they	saw	the Crown Jewels.
When they	visited	the Tower they	saw	the Crown Jewels.

Kurzgrammatik

When	–	–	coming	to the party you	**will**	meet a lot of friends.
When you	**will**		come	to the party you	will	meet a lot of friends.

Wird der Nebensatz mit "after" eingeleitet, so solltest Du immer past perfect verwenden. (Zeitenfolge NS: past perfect – HS: past tense).

d) Ist der verkürzte **Nebensatz verneint**, so mußt Du bei der Auflösung mit einer Form von "to do" umschreiben. Ausnahme: wenn ein Hilfszeitwort im Satz steht.

–	–	–	**Not**	having	much practice John failed the examination.
As he		**did**	**not**	have	much practice John failed the examination.
–	–		**Not**	being	good he failed the exam.
As he				**wasn't**	good he failed the exam.

6. Auflösung einer Satzreihe

Ein Partizip kann auch zwei oder mehrere **Hauptsätze** verbinden. Dabei werden immer gleichzeitige Handlungen beschrieben. *Beachte* deshalb folgende Punkte:

a) Verbinde die Hauptsätze durch "and" oder Kommata, falls es mehrere Hauptsätze sind.

b) Ergänze in den aufgelösten Hauptsätzen das Subjekt des ersten Hauptsatzes.

c) Löse das Partizip auf und setze das daraus entstehende Verb in dieselbe Zeit, in der das Verb des ersten Hauptsatzes steht.

He sat in his chair	–	–	**holding**	the newspaper in his hands.
He sat in his chair	**and**	**(he)**	**held**	the newspaper in his hands.
	a	b	c	

Passive Voice – Das Passiv

Eine Handlung kann im Aktiv oder im Passiv beschrieben werden. Während im Aktiv (Tatform) das Subjekt des Satzes handelt, wird im Passiv (Leideform) mit dem Subjekt etwas gemacht.

Bildung	eine Form von **to be** + **past participle**	**Aktiv:** Columbus discovered America. → **Passiv:** America was discovered by Columbus.

1. Umwandlung vom Aktiv ins Passiv

Beachte bei der Umwandlung vom Aktiv ins Passiv folgende Punkte:

a) Als erstes bestimmst Du **Subjekt und Objekt des Aktivsatzes**. Das Subjekt des Aktivsatzes wird zum Objekt des Passivsatzes, das Objekt des Aktivsatzes wird zum Subjekt des Passivsatzes.

b) Das Objekt im Passivsatz muß mit "**by**" (im Deutschen: von) angeschlossen werden.

	S	P	O	
Aktiv:	They	kick	the ball.	
Passiv:	The ball	is kicked	by	them.
	Der Ball	wird	von	ihnen	geschossen.

c) Als nächstes bestimmst Du die **Zeit** des **Aktivsatzes**. Diese verwandeltst Du dann in die entsprechende Zeit im Passiv.
Lerne für die Umwandlung folgende Tabelle:

	Aktiv:		**Passiv:**	
Simple Present:	I	paint the wall.	It is	painted.
Present Progressive:	I am	painting it.	It is being	painted.
Simple Past:	I	painted it.	It was	painted.
Past Progressive:	I was	painting it.	It was being	painted.
Present Perfect:	I have	painted it.	It has been	painted.
Past Perfect:	I had	painted it.	It had been	painted.
Future I:	I will	paint it.	It will be	painted.
Future II:	I will have	painted it.	It will have been	painted.
Conditional I:	I would	paint it.	It would be	painted.
Conditional II:	I would have	painted it.	It would have been	painted.

d) Sind im Aktivsatz **zwei Objekte** (Objekt im Dativ = O_3/Objekt im Akkusativ = O_4) vorhanden, so kannst Du zwei verschiedene Passivsätze bilden, indem Du jeweils ein Objekt zum Subjekt des Passivsatzes machst, während Du das zweite Objekt unverändert stehen läßt. *Beachte* allerdings: O_3 muß im Passivsatz mit "to" angeschlossen werden.

		O_3	O_4	
Aktiv:	They offered	him	a job.	
Passiv:		↓		
1. Mögl.:		He	was offered	a job.
2. Mögl.:			A job	was offered to him.

Englische Passivsätze werden im Deutschen oft durch einen Aktivsatz mit "man" wiedergegeben.

It **is said** that he earned a lot of money.   **Man** sagt, daß er viel Geld verdient habe.
Nothing **can be done** against it.   **Man** kann nichts dagegen machen.

2. Umwandlung vom Passiv ins Aktiv

a) **Unterstreiche** im Passivsatz das Subjekt und Objekt, das mit "by" angeschlossen ist. Das Objekt wird im Aktivsatz zum Subjekt, und das Subjekt des Passivsatzes wird zum Objekt des Aktivsatzes.

b) Das "by" im Passivsatz fällt im Aktivsatz weg.

	S				O
Passiv:	He	was	asked	by	the teacher.
Aktiv:	The teacher		asked	–	him.

c) Als nächstes bestimmst Du die **Zeit** des Passivsatzes und überträgst sie in den Aktivsatz. Siehe dazu die Tabelle S. G 21.

d) Nun überprüfst Du, ob das neue Subjekt im Aktivsatz im **Singular** oder **Plural** steht. Entsprechend mußt Du die Verbform angleichen.

Passiv:	They	**have**	been asked	by	the teacher.
		↓			
Aktiv:	The teacher	has		asked		them.

e) Ist im Passivsatz **kein Handelnder mit "by"** angegeben, so mußt Du sinngemäß einen Handelnden ergänzen und zum Subjekt des Aktivsatzes machen. Du kannst dabei **"allgemeine" Subjekte** verwenden wie **"people, they, you, we"** oder ein Substantiv, das inhaltlich paßt.

Passiv:	School uniforms	are worn		in Britain	.
Aktiv:	Boys and girls	wear	school uniforms	in Britain.	

Reciprocal Pronoun – Das Fürwort der Gegenseitigkeit

Das reziproke Pronomen **each other** = **one another** bleibt in allen Personen unverändert.

1. Reziproker Gebrauch

Wir verwenden "each other" für das deutsche "sich", wenn **mehrere verschiedene Personen** etwas tun. Im Deutschen kann für das "sich" auch **"einander, gegenseitig"** eingesetzt werden. Um Fehler zu vermeiden, solltest Du immer die **Einsetzprobe** machen!

She smiles at him. ⎫
He smiles at her. ⎭ They smile at **each other**.

2. Unterschiede zum Deutschen

Nach bestimmten Verben **entfällt "each other"**, auch wenn im Deutschen "sich" steht. Lerne diese Verben!

to meet	sich treffen	to fall in love	sich verlieben
to kiss	sich küssen	to become engaged	sich verloben
to quarrel	sich streiten	to get married	sich (ver)heiraten
to part	sich trennen	to get a divorce	sich scheiden lassen

Unsicherheiten entstehen oft, wenn man sich entscheiden soll zwischen "oneself" und "each other", da beide Ausdrücke im Deutschen mit "sich" wiedergegeben werden. Deshalb merke Dir den wesentlichsten **Unterschied** zwischen "reflexive" und "reciprocal pronoun":

Reflexive Pronoun	bezieht sich auf **ein und dieselbe Person**
Reciprocal Pronoun	**mehrere Personen** sind beteiligt; *Einsetzprobe:* einander, gegenseitig

Kurzgrammatik

Reflexive Pronoun – Das rückbezügliche Fürwort

Das Reflexivpronomen im Englischen ist eine Form von **oneself**. Im Deutschen wird es mit "sich" übersetzt.

Singular: myself
yourself
himself
herself
itself

Plural: ourselves
yourselves
themselves

1. Reflexiver Gebrauch

Das Reflexivpronomen darf nur verwendet werden, wenn Subjekt und Objekt im Satz **ein und dieselbe Person** sind. Es heißt eben deswegen "rückbezügliches Fürwort", weil es sich auf das Subjekt im Satz zurückbezieht.

S		O		
Mr. Smith	sees	himself	in the mirror.	**S = O**

2. Unterschiede zum Deutschen

Schwierigkeiten bei der Anwendung ergeben sich dadurch, daß es einige englische Verben gibt, die **keine Form von "oneself"** nach sich ziehen, obwohl im Deutschen "sich" steht. Dazu gehören u. a.

to apologize	sich entschuldigen	to lie down	sich hinlegen
to argue	sich streiten	to meet	sich treffen
to change	sich (ver)ändern	to move	sich bewegen
to complain	sich beklagen	to open	sich öffnen
to differ from	sich unterscheiden	to refer to	sich beziehen auf
to feel	sich fühlen	to refuse	sich weigern
to happen	sich ereignen	to relax	sich entspannen
to hide	sich verstecken	to remember	sich erinnern,
to hurry (up)	sich beeilen		sich merken
to imagine	sich (etwas) vorstellen	to wonder	sich fragen
to join	sich anschließen	to worry	sich Sorgen machen

3. Bedeutung unterschiedlich

Es gibt nun Verben, die als Objekt **sowohl ein Substantiv als auch ein Reflexivpronomen** nach sich haben können. Dabei verändert sich allerdings die **Wortbedeutung!** Lerne diese Ausdrücke!

to enjoy	the party	die Party **genießen**
to enjoy	oneself	sich **amüsieren**
to help	a person	jemandem **helfen**
to help	oneself to the milk	sich mit Milch **bedienen**
to occupy	a town	eine Stadt **besetzen**
to occupy	oneself with a book	sich mit einem Buch **beschäftigen**
to control	the traffic	den Verkehr **kontrollieren**
to control	oneself	sich **beherrschen**

4. verstärkender Gebrauch

Das **verstärkende Pronomen** hat dieselben Formen wie das Reflexivpronomen. Im Deutschen wird es mit "selbst, selber" wiedergegeben. Das verstärkende Pronomen **hebt** das vorausgehende Substantiv oder Pronomen **besonders hervor**.

He prepared this delicious meal **himself**.

Relative Clauses – Relativsätze

Man unterscheidet im Englischen zwei Arten von Relativsätzen, nämlich den nicht notwendigen oder nichtbestimmenden (non-defining) Relativsatz und den notwendigen oder bestimmenden (defining) Relativsatz.

1. Nichtbestimmende Relativsätze (Non-defining Relative Clauses)

Nichtbestimmende Relativsätze ergänzen den Hauptsatz durch eine **Zusatzinformation**, die **nicht** unbedingt **notwendig** ist für das Verständnis des Hauptsatzes. Sie müssen durch ein **Komma** vom Hauptsatz abgetrennt werden.

a) das Relativpronomen bei Personen

Nominativ	Peter, **who** lives in London, visits his uncle.
Genitiv	Peter, **whose** parents are rather old, plays chess.
Präposition + Dativ	Peter, **to whom** Tom owes a lot of money, is angry.
Akkusativ	Peter, **whom** I met yesterday, joined a club.

b) das Relativpronomen bei Dingen

Nominativ	This room, **which** is our classroom, is new.
Genitiv	This room, **whose** walls are yellow, is rather small.
Präposition + Dativ	This room, **in which** we are, is full of pupils.
Akkusativ	This room, **which** you see, must be tidied.

2. Bestimmende/notwendige Relativsätze (Defining Relative Clauses)

Bestimmende Relativsätze bestimmen den Inhalt des Hauptsatzes näher. Sie geben **wichtige Informationen** und sind deshalb notwendig für das Verständnis des Satzes. Sie dürfen nicht durch ein Komma abgetrennt werden.

a) das Relativpronomen bei Personen

Nominativ	The girl	**who** opens the door **that**	is Mary Parker.
Genitiv	The girl	**whose** bike was stolen	is very sad.
Präposition + Dativ	The girl	**for whom** we are waiting **whom** we are waiting **for** **who** we are waiting **for** **that** we are waiting **for** – we are waiting **for**	is late.
Akkusativ	The girl	**whom** we met **who** we met **that** we met – we met	is nice.

b) das Relativpronomen bei Dingen

Nominativ	The book	**which** is red **that**	is from the library.
Genitiv	The book	**whose** cover is red	is very old.
Präposition + Dativ	The book	**with which** we work **which** we work **with** **that** we work **with** – we work **with**	is interesting.
Akkusativ	The book	**which** I bought yesterday **that** I bought – I bought	was rather cheap.

Reported Speech – Indirekte Rede

1. Umwandlung von direkter in indirekte Rede

Eine beliebte Aufgabenstellung innerhalb der Grammatik ist die Umwandlung von der direkten in die indirekte Rede. Grundsätzlich ist bei der Umwandlung von direkter zu indirekter Rede folgendes zu beachten:

a) Veränderung des Subjekts

Direkte Rede:	He says,	"I ↓	am	tired."
Indirekte Rede:	He says (that)	he	is	tired.

b) Veränderung des Possessivpronomens (besitzanzeigendes Fürwort)

Direkte Rede:	He says,	"I	close	my ↓	book."
Indirekte Rede:	He says (that)	he	closes	his	book.

c) Veränderung der Zeit des Verbs, wenn das "reporting verb" (Verb des Berichtens, z. B. say) in einer Zeit der Vergangenheit steht.

Verb in	Direkte Rede		Indirekte Rede
	Simple Present	→	Simple Past
	Simple Past	→	Simple Past
	oder	→	Past Perfect
	Present Perfect	→	Past Perfect
	Past Perfect	→	Past Perfect
	Future I	→	Conditional I
	Future Perfect	→	Conditional Perfect

Direkte Rede:	He said,	"I	shall (will) ↓	leave."
Indirekte Rede:	He said	that he	would	leave.

Beachte: Steht das "reporting verb" in der Gegenwart, so bleibt die Zeit des Verbs erhalten.

Direkte Rede:	He says,	"I	will (shall)	leave."
			↓	
Indirekte Rede:	He says that	he	will	leave.

d) Veränderung von Adverbien

Direkte Rede:	→	Indirekte Rede:
now	→	then
here	→	there
this	→	that
yesterday	→	the day before
tomorrow	→	the next day
next week	→	the following week
ago	→	before
today	→	that day

e) Der **Befehl** wird in der indirekten Rede als "object + infinitive" wiedergegeben. Das "reporting verb" "say" muß zu "tell" werden.

Direkte Rede:	I	said	to him,	"Open		the window."
		↓				
Indirekte Rede:	I	told	– him	to	open	the window.

f) Der **verneinte Befehl** erscheint als "object + negative infinitive". Die Umschreibung mit "do, does" fällt weg.

Direkte Rede:	I said	to him	"Do	not		open	the window."
Indirekte Rede:	I told	him	–	not	to	open	the window.

g) Bei der Umwandlung der direkten **Frage** in die indirekte mußt Du folgendes beachten:

- Ist die Frage mit einem **Fragewort** (who, when, where, what, how ...) eingeleitet, so bleibt dieses erhalten. Es ändert sich nur die Satzstellung in der indirekten Frage.

Direkte Frage: Prädikat – Subjekt – Objekt (P – S – O)
Indirekte Frage: Subjekt – Prädikat – Objekt (S – P – O)

(Satzstellung wie im Aussagesatz)

Kurzgrammatik

		P	S		
Direkte Rede:	He asked me,	"What	is	your name?	
Indirekte Rede:	He asked me	what	–	my name	was.
			S		P

- Ist **kein Fragewort** vorhanden, so mußt Du die indirekte Frage mit **"if"** oder **"whether"** einleiten.

Direkte Rede:	He asked us,	–	"Are	you	hungry?"
Indirekte Rede:	He asked us	**whether**		we were	hungry.

- Die **Umschreibung** mit "do, does, did" entfällt bei der Umwandlung:

Direkte Rede:	He asked us,	"Why	do	you	leave	the party?
Indirekte Rede:	He asked us	why	–	we	left	the party.

Ansonsten gelten die Regeln a–d

2. Umwandlung von indirekter in direkte Rede

a) Indirekter Aussagesatz

Dabei mußt Du dieselben Regeln beachten wie bei der Verwandlung in die indirekte Rede, nur eben in umgekehrter Reihenfolge.
Wichtig ist, daß Du als erstes immer beachtest, in welcher Zeit das "reporting verb" (Verb des Berichtens) steht. Steht es in der Gegenwart, mußt Du die Zeit des Verbs beibehalten, steht es in einer Vergangenheit, mußt Du die Zeit des Verbs verwandeln!

Indirekte Rede:	She said	she	would sell	her	car	the next day.
		↓	↓	↓		↓
Direkte Rede:	She said,	"I	will sell (shall)	my	car	tomorrow."

b) Indirekter Fragesatz

Es gelten die Regeln a–d.
Beachte:
- Das Fragewort bleibt erhalten.
- Ist die indirekte Frage mit "if" oder "whether" eingeleitet, so fällt dieses bei der Rückwandlung weg.
- Umschreibe mit einer Form von "to do" (do, does, did), außer wenn ein Hilfszeitwort (is, are, was, were, can, could, must, may ...) im Satz steht.

Indirekte Frage:	She asks	whether	–	he	came	the day before.
Direkte Frage:	She asks,	–	"Did	you	come	yesterday?"

Subject and Object Questions – Fragen nach dem Subjekt und dem Objekt

Bei den Subjekt- und Objektfragen ist es wichtig, daß Du den Satz nach Subjekt (Satzgegenstand im 1. Fall = wer oder was?) bzw. Objekt (Satzaussage im 3. Fall = wem? oder im 4. Fall = wen oder was?) abfragst, damit Du die folgenden Regeln anwenden kannst. Auch die Zeit, in der der Satz steht, mußt Du beibehalten.

1. Fragen nach dem Subjekt: "who" oder "what" = wer oder was?

a) nach Personen

Gegenwart	They visit the Tower. **Who** visits the Tower?	Sie besuchen den Tower. **Wer** besucht den Tower? **1. Fall**: Frage nach dem Subjekt
1. Vergangenheit	They visited the Tower. **Who** visited the Tower?	

b) nach Dingen

Gegenwart	The pear-tree grows in our garden. **What** grows in our garden?	Der Birnbaum wächst in unserem Garten. **Was** wächst in unserem Garten? **1. Fall**: Frage nach dem Subjekt
1. Vergangenheit	The pear-tree grew in our garden. **What** grew in our garden?	

Merke: Wenn nach dem Subjekt (Satzgegenstand = 1. Fall) des Satzes gefragt wird, so darf **nicht** mit einer **Form von "do"** umschrieben werden. Das Verb muß gebeugt werden, d. h. in der Gegenwart muß es mit dem 3. Person-s, in der Vergangenheit mit der Vergangenheitsendung gekennzeichnet werden.

Kurzgrammatik

2. Fragen nach dem Objekt: "whom = who" oder "what" = wen oder was?

a) nach Personen

Gegenwart	I know Jenny. (her) Whom/Who do I know?	I kenne Jenny. (sie) Wen kenne ich? **4. Fall**: Frage nach dem Akkusativobjekt
1. Vergangenheit	I knew Jenny. Whom/Who did I know?	

b) nach Dingen

Gegenwart	She buys a dress. **What does** she buy?	Sie kauft ein Kleid. **Was** kauft sie? **4. Fall**: Frage nach dem Akkusativobjekt
1. Vergangenheit	She bought a dress. **What did** she buy?	

Merke: Bei Fragen nach dem Objekt mußt Du mit **"do/does"** in der Gegenwart und mit **"did"** in der 1. Vergangenheit umschreiben.

3. Fragen nach dem Objekt mit Präposition (Verhältniswort): "to whom = who ... to?" "to what = what ... to?"

Viele englische Verben ziehen ein Verhältniswort nach sich, das im Deutschen nicht auftritt, sondern durch den 3. Fall (Dativ) wiedergegeben wird.

a) nach Personen

Gegenwart	This book belongs **to** me. **To whom does** this book belong? **Who does** this book belong **to**?	Dieses Buch gehört mir. **Wem** gehört dieses Buch? **3. Fall**: im Englischen mit Verhältniswort – Frage nach dem Objekt mit Präposition
1. Vergangenheit	This book belong**ed to** me. **To whom did** this book belong? **Who did** this book belong **to**?	

G 32

b) nach Dingen

Gegenwart	I listen **to** music. **To what do** I listen? **What do** I listen **to**?	Ich höre der Musik zu. **Wem** höre ich zu? **3. Fall:** im Englischen mit Verhältniswort – Frage nach dem Objekt mit Verhältniswort
1. Vergangenheit	I listen**ed** to music. **To what did** I listen? **What did** I listen **to**?	

Merke: Bei der Frage nach dem Präpositionalobjekt (Objekt mit Verhältniswort) muß ebenfalls mit **"do/does"** bzw. **"did"** umschrieben werden. Die Präposition kann dabei entweder **vor** dem Fragewort (who, what) oder **am Ende** des Satzes stehen.

Kurzgrammatik

Tenses – Die Zeiten

Im Grammatikteil der Abschlußprüfungen sind oft Einsetzübungen verlangt, bei denen Du das Verb in die richtige Zeit setzen mußt. Wiederhole dazu eigenständig die Bildung der englischen Zeiten. Für die Anwendung der englischen Zeiten merke Dir grundsätzlich

> Sogenannte Signalwörter zeigen Dir oft an, welche Zeit Du verwenden mußt. Präge sie Dir genau ein!

Für die Bildung bestimmter Zeiten brauchst Du z. T. das "present participle" bzw. das "past participle". Zur Bildung und Schreibweise siehe S. G 16.

1. Simple Present/Present Tense

Bildung	entspricht der Grundform (dem Infinitiv) des Verbs	I usually **carry** the parcel to the post office.
	Beachte: Umschreibung mit **do/does** in **Frage** und **Verneinung**, wenn das Prädikat aus einem Vollverb besteht.	He **doesn't** carry .../I **don't** carry ... **Does** he carry ...?/**Do** you carry ...? **Doesn't** he carry ...?/ **Don't** you carry ...?
Verwendung	Es beschreibt	
	• **Gewohnheiten**, sich wiederholende Handlungen	I **read** the newspaper **every day**. *Signalwörter:* always, every day, every week, sometimes, usually, often, never
	• **allgemeingültige Aussagen, Wahrheiten**	The sun **rises** in the east.
	• **Gedanken, Gefühle**, ausgedrückt durch bestimmte Verben	I **think** it's wonderful. *weitere Verben:* to like, to want, to believe, to think, to mean, to know, to understand
	• **Zustände**, ausgedrückt durch bestimmte Verben	This book **belongs to** Tony. *weitere Verben:* to belong, to cost, to own, to need, to seem, to remember, to forget

2. Present Progressive/Present Continuous

Bildung	to be + present participle (am/is/are + -ing-Form)	He **is** just read**ing** a book. He **isn't** read**ing** a book. **Is** he read**ing** a book? **Isn't** he read**ing** a book?
Verwendung	• Handlungen, die **gerade** geschehen	He is **just** reading a book. *Signalwörter:* just, now, at this moment
	• Handlungen, die **für die Zukunft** schon fest **geplant** sind	I am flying to New York **next weekend**. I have already got the tickets.

3. Simple Past/Past Tense

Bildung	• bei den **regelmäßigen** Verben: -ed an die Grundform des Verbs	I talk**ed** to him yesterday.
	y → i stummes -e fällt weg Verdoppelung des **Konsonanten** am Wortende nach kurzem, betontem Vokal	marry → married believe → believed drop → dropped
	• vgl. Liste der **unregelmäßigen** Verben in Deinem Schulbuch (2. Verbform)	I **wrote** a letter.
	Beachte: Umschreibung mit **"did"** in **Frage** und **Verneinung**	I **didn't** talk to him. **Did** you talk to him? **Didn't** you talk to him?

Verwendung	• Handlungen, die (in der Vergangenheit) **bereits abgeschlossen** sind	They moved to London **in 1982**.
	• Ereignisse einer Erzählung, die **bereits vergangen** sind	They packed their things into suitcases, loaded the car und left for Ireland. *Signalwörter:* yesterday, last week, last year, in 1934, ago, this morning (wenn bereits Nachmittag ist), Fragen mit "when", "what time"

4. Past Progressive / Past Continuous

Bildung	was/were + present participle (ing-form)	He **was** (not) writ**ing** a letter.

Verwendung	• wenn der **Vorgang** der Handlung, nicht das Ergebnis interessiert	He was reading a book.
	• Handlung, die zu einem Zeitpunkt in der **Vergangenheit noch nicht abgeschlossen** war	What were you doing **at 3 o'clock yesterday** afternoon?

5. Present Perfect

Bildung	have/has + past participle	I **have** just finish**ed** my homework.

Verwendung	• wenn eine Handlung in der Vergangenheit begonnen hat, aber **in der Gegenwart noch andauert,** noch nicht abgeschlossen ist	I haven't met him **since** last Monday. *Signalwörter:* for, how long, since etc.
	• wenn das **Ergebnis** einer kürzlich stattgefundenen Handlung **sichtbar** ist	I have **just** washed the cups. They are clean **now**. *Signalwort:* just

• wenn etwas **schon einmal** oder (bis jetzt) **noch nie** geschehen ist	Have you **ever** been to England? *Signalwörter:* already, always, before, ever, yet (immer am Schluß des Satzes), never, not ... yet, often, so far, up till now
• wenn ein Ereignis während eines **noch nicht abgeschlossenen Zeitraums** stattfindet	I haven't seen him **today**. *Signalwörter:* this morning/week, today

Beachte den Gebrauch von "since" und "for"

Beide Wörter werden im Deutschen mit "seit" übersetzt!

since gibt den **Beginn** einer Handlung, einen **Zeitpunkt** an.	I haven't seen him since 1971. since last Friday. since 3 o'clock.
for bezeichnet die **Dauer** eines Zustands, den **Zeitraum**.	I have known him for 3 years. for a long time. for some months.
Beachte: Im Deutschen steht häufig die Gegenwart.	Ich kenne ihn seit 3 Jahren.

6. Present Perfect Progressive

Bildung	have/has + been + present participle (ing-Form)	I **have been** wait**ing** for 3 hours now.
Verwendung	Handlungen, die in der **Vergangenheit begonnen haben** und bis in die **Gegenwart andauern**. Im Deutschen wird diese Zeit oft durch Präsens wiedergegeben.	Ich warte **schon** seit drei Stunden.

G 37

7. Past Perfect

Bildung	had + past participle	I arrived at the station after the train **had left**.
Verwendung	Wenn eine Handlung in der Vergangenheit (1) abgeschlossen wurde vor einer anderen Handlung (2) in der Vergangenheit. Past perfect tritt häufig in Verbindung mit past tense auf.	She had finished her letter (1) when the telephone rang. (2)

8. Past Perfect Progressive

Bildung	had been + present participle (ing-Form)	I had a bad cough because I **had been** walk**ing** in the rain for two hours until I decided to go in.
Verwendung	Handlung, die bis zu einem Zeitpunkt in der Vergangenheit andauerte.	

9. Future

Es gibt, je nach Absicht, verschiedene Möglichkeiten, die Zukunft auszudrücken.

a) will-future

Bildung	will/shall + infinitive (Grundform des Verbs)	Tomorrow the weather **will be** sunny.

Kurzgrammatik

Verwendung	• Ereignisse in der Zukunft, **auf die wir keinen Einfluß** haben	It will be very hot.
	• Handlungen, zu denen wir uns **im Augenblick des Sprechens entschließen**	I think I'll (will/shall) watch TV this evening.

b) going-to-future

Bildung	to be going to + infinitive	He **is going to** take part in the football match.

Verwendung	• Handlungen, die man zu tun **beabsichtigt**	I am going to study at Exeter.
	• **Vorhersagen** über die Zukunft aufgrund **äußerer Anzeichen**	Look at these clouds. It's going to rain.

c) Present Progressive

Bildung	to be + present participle (ing-Form)	We **are** watch**ing** the Davis Cup next week. I have already got the tickets.

Verwendung	Handlungen, die für die Zukunft **geplant** sind.	*Signalwörter:* tomorrow, next week, next month, soon, tonight, this evening, afterwards

d) Future Progressive

Bildung	will + be + present participle (ing-Form)	I'**ll be** read**ing** all evening.

Verwendung	Handlungen, die **zu einem Zeitpunkt** in der Zukunft ablaufen werden.	I think I will be travelling to New York next year.

G 39

e) Future Perfect (oder Future II)

Bildung	will have + past participle	He **will have** reach**ed** England tomorrow by 9 o'clock.

Verwendung	Handlungen, die **zu einem bestimmten Zeitpunkt** in der Zukunft **abgeschlossen,** vollendet sein werden	*Signalwörter:* by then, before tomorrow, by + bestimmte Zeitangabe

10. Conditional I

Bildung	would + infinitive	He **would take** part in the race.

Verwendung	wenn eine Handlung unter einer bestimmten Bedingung eintreten würde

11. Conditional Perfect/Conditional II

Bildung	would + have + past participle	He **would have bought** the house.

Verwendung	wenn etwas unter einer bestimmten Bedingung geschehen wäre

**Realschulabschluss Englisch in Mecklenburg-Vorpommern
Probearbeit 1997**

Fast Food – Big Money

McDonald's is certainly the biggest name in the fast food business, and, more than that, it is a new way of eating, a new way of life for millions of people, not only in America. For most people "fast food" is typically American. It started in America in 1954 when Ray Kroc, the real "ideas man" and owner of McDonald's, first met the McDonald brothers at
5 their hamburger stand in San Bernardino, California.
What makes fast food places like McDonald's so popular? In the first place they are what their name says they are – fast. At McDonald's, they say, you never have to wait longer than 60 seconds for your order. Secondly, they are cheaper than restaurants – even a father of four can usually afford to take his family out for a meal if he goes to a fast food shop.
10 And for teenagers it is a popular meeting (and eating) place before the disco or after the cinema. Thirdly, they are all almost clinically clean. And – you can get not only hamburgers there, as in the early days, but also chicken, sea food, pizza, tacos and pancakes.
This is certainly big business for the people who own the fast food shops, but what about the people who work there? Most of them are students or housewives who like the flexible
15 working hours: the shops are open from early in the morning (sometimes 5.30 a.m.) until late at night (often 1 a.m. at weekends). But the pay is not very good and often they have to accept difficult working conditions such as night work, stress, no special security.
And there is not much time to talk to the customers, who usually leave after no longer than 15 minutes, anyway. There are no cigarette machines, no jukeboxes, no fruit machines; the
20 atmosphere is as aseptic as the food: no quiet corners, no comfortable seats, no wine list, nothing to make the place interesting *after* the meal. But this is not what the typical fast food customer is looking for, it seems. "The food is good, and it's fast," says a young father who is enjoying a meal with his daughter. "It was her idea to come here." And a 21-year-old student, who is enjoying the Quarter Pounders, says, "You know what you're
25 getting when you come to McDonald's." And this is perhaps the most important thing for McDonald's customers in more than 30 countries today.

Quelle: TAKE OFF 1, Cornelsen & Oxford, Berlin. 1. Auflage 1991.

Aufgaben

I. Comprehension

1. Matching exercise. Combine the matching parts of the sentences. (6 p.)

   (1) McDonald's is the biggest name
   (2) Lots of people think fast food
   (3) People go to McDonald's
   (4) It is a popular meeting place for teenagers
   (5) People who work there
   (6) There is nothing

   a) haven't got enough time to talk with the customers.
   b) because it's cheaper than other restaurants.
   c) in the fast food business.
   d) is typical of America.
   e) to make the place interesting to stay there after a meal.
   f) before they go to the disco.

   Put the correct letters below the numbers:

(1)	(2)	(3)	(4)	(5)	(6)

2. Read the text carefully. Find out which statements are true and which are false. Mark with a cross. (8 p.)

true	false	
		a) McDonald's started to sell fast food in Hamburg 40 years ago.
		b) McDonald's is called after its owner.
		c) You can get your food very quickly there.
		d) In the fifties, people could get chicken and pizza at McDonald's.
		e) The owners of fast food restaurants make a lot of money.
		f) The working conditions at McDonald's are excellent.
		g) People like McDonald's because they can sit there comfortably.
		h) You can't drink wine at McDonald's.

II. Language

From the 20 words below choose the suitable ones and fill in the gaps. (10 p.)

popular – households – However – employs – healthy – remains – afford – buildings – turned away – everywhere – atmosphere – sign – although – Consumers – interesting – offer – owners – which – recommended – business

Americans have become more and more interested in eating (1) _____ food. Many Americans have (2) _____ from their traditional meat and potato diet and started eating more salads, fruits and vegetables. Margarine and vegetable oil have replaced butter and bacon fat in many (3)

2

_____. Nowadays people are much more careful about sugar, (4) _____ is responsible for tooth decay and weight problems. (5) _____ are now demanding sugar-free soft drinks and sweeteners for tea, coffee and desserts. Alcohol, as in many countries, (6) _____ a problem. (7) _____, even here the trend is away from 'hard' spirits towards wine, low-calorie beer and alcohol-free cocktails. Perhaps the clearest (8) _____ of this change in eating habits is found in restaurants. Most of them are trying very hard to (9) _____ low-fat, low-salt and low-calorie food. There are now salad bars (10) _____, full of fresh fruit and vegetables, even in fast food restaurants.

III. Grammar

1. Fill in the correct words. (8 p.)

noun	verb	adjective
cleanliness		
	realize	
speciality		
		acceptable

2. Adjective or adverb? Put in the correct forms. (5 p.)

   a) Eating at McDonald's is very _____, especially for young people. (popular)

   b) People needn't wait _____ for their meals. (impatient)

   c) The meals are _____. (delicious)

   d) But the people who are employed there must work _____. (hard)

   e) They are not _____ paid. (good)

3. If clauses. Please fill in the correct forms. (3 p.)

   a) If you go to McDonald's, you _____ a lot of young people. (meet)

   b) I would eat there more often, if I _____ more pocket-money. (get)

   c) If I had more time after school, I _____ in a fast food restaurant. (work)

4. Reported speech. The following discussion was printed in a daily paper. The readers spoke out on fast food and the intention to build another McDonald's restaurant in their town. Report what they said. (9 p.)

   Miss Jones declared, "I don't like fast food and places like McDonald's."
   Mr Miller asked, "Will it be better to have another McDonald's?"
   Mrs Smith answered, "But the old shop is often overcrowded."

Liz & Andrew said, "A new McDonald's – that can be super. It seems to be the most popular meeting place for many youngsters. We met there 6 weeks ago and have been in love since then."

Miss Jones declared that she _____

_____

_____

_____

_____

_____

_____

_____

_____

_____

_____

_____

5. Please put the verbs in brackets into the correct tense. (8 p.)

Last week I got a letter from a British pen-friend who wrote about the latest attraction in his small town: Another American fast food chain, 'Pizza-Hut', _____ just _____ (open) its first restaurant in Widdington. Of course, I went there because I _____ (be) interested in what they _____ (have) to offer. I found out that I _____ (not like) the Giant Superburger, but I _____ never _____ (taste) better french fries before. While most people around me _____ (drink) coca-cola light, I _____ (order) a simple milk-shake – nothing extraordinary. Despite its quickness, I think this fast food place _____ (not see) me again very soon.

IV. Using the language in different contexts

Defective dialogue. (18 p.)

You overhear the conversation between an old woman and a young girl at McDonald's, but you can't understand everything they say. Please complete the dialogue.

old woman: Excuse me, do you often come here?

young girl: _____

_____

_____

old woman: I've never been here before. But today I'm a bit short of time, and I'm very hungry.

young girl: _____

_____

_____

young girl: Well, I work in an office not far from here. There's only half an hour for lunch and the service is fast here. Also, it's cheap for me.

old woman: _____

_____

young girl: Yes, I do. I think there's a big variety of food. I do not only have hamburgers. I especially like chicken.

old woman: But I think the food isn't very healthy, is it?

young girl: _____

_____

old woman: Can you help me with my order, then? I don't know what to take.

young girl: _____

_____

old woman: _____

_____

(12 contents, 6 correctness)

V. Comment

Comment on *two* of the following statements. Write about 80 words altogether. Count your words. (20 p.)

1. Young people don't know enough about the risks of eating too much fast food.
2. Fast food restaurants are not a good place for a romantic evening.
3. McDonald's is certainly big business for some people.
4. "All my friends go to McDonald's, so I go with them, but I don't like it."
5. At McDonald's you can't buy alcoholic drinks with your meal. That makes it a good place for young people.
6. "Chips! I'm doing the *Slimfast*[1] diet at the moment. *Slimfast* and chips is good." (Robbie Williams)

[1] a drink which is said to make you lose weight.

(10 contents, 10 correctness)

VI. Giving opinion

The following statement was taken from a letter to the editor of a sports magazine: "Fast food is booming. We are a nation of lazy, unhealthy people."

Do you agree or not? Give reasons. You might think of: calories, health, dangers, costs, friends, parents, spare time, fitness clubs, teenage magazines, fashion, eating habits, couch potatoes etc.

Write about 150 words altogether. Count your words. (25 p.)

(15 contents, 10 correctness)

Lösung

I. Comprehension

1.

(1)	(2)	(3)	(4)	(5)	(6)
c	d	b	f	a	e

2. a) false   b) false
   c) true   d) false
   e) true   f) false
   g) false   h) true

II. Language

(1) healthy, (2) turned away, (3) households, (4) which, (5) Consumers, (6) remains, (7) However, (8) sign, (9) offer, (10) everywhere

III. Grammar

1.

noun	verb	adjective
cleanliness	to clean	clean
realization	to realize	realizable
speciality	to specialize	special
acceptance	to accept	acceptable

2. a) popular   b) impatiently
   c) delicious   d) hard
   e) well

3. a) ..., you **will meet** a lot of ...
   (Hinweis: Hauptsatz = Simple Future Typ 1)
   b) ... if I **got** more ...
   (Hinweis: Nebensatz = Simple Past Typ 2)
   c) ..., I **would work** in a ...
   (Hinweis: Hauptsatz = would + Infinitive Typ 2)

4. Antworten in folgender Reihenfolge
   Miss Jones declared that she **didn't like** fast food and places like McDonald's.
   Mr Miller asked if it **would be** better to have another McDonald's.
   Mrs Smith anwered that the old shop **was** often overcrowded.
   Liz and Andrew said that a new McDonald's **could** be super.
   It **seemed** to be the most popular meeting place for many youngsters.
   They had met there 6 weeks ago and **had been** in love since then.

5. Antworten in folgender Reihenfolge

has just **opened**
(Hinweis: Simple Present Perfect)

was interested in what they **had** to offer.
(Hinweis: Simple Past)

didn't like ... **had** never **tasted** ...
(Hinweis: Simple Past, Simple Past Perfect)

... **were drinking** ... **ordered**
(Hinweis: Past Progressive, Simple Past)

... **won't see** ...
(Hinweis: Simple Future)

IV. Using the language in different contexts

young girl: "Yes I do. I come here almost every day."
young girl: "Why do you come here so often?"
old woman: "Do you like this fast food?"
young girl: "Oh, you can choose between fatty, not so healthy meals like hamburgers or chips and salad, chicken, or seafood which are delicious and healthy."
young girl: "Of course, I can. I would advise you to take the fresh salad with chicken."
old woman: "Thank you very much. It was nice to meet you."

V. Comment

1. Young people don't know enough about the risks of eating too much fast food.
   I'm afraid I have to agree. Young people are not aware of the risks of eating too much fast food. They do not know that fast food is often of poor quality and not very healthy. Although a lot of meals are fatty, for example hamburgers or chips, fast food is very popular with young people because it is cheap. They don't worry very much about health factors.

2. Fast food restaurants are not a good place for a romantic evening.
   I agree with this statement. Fast food restaurants are so popular because of their informal atmosphere. That's why they cannot be the right place for a romantic evening with a good dinner and candle light. Customers queuing up for their meals, people serving you from behind the counters instead of waiters, uncomfortable chairs, and tables without a tablecloth do not create an atmosphere for a romantic evening.

3. McDonald's is certainly big business for some people.
   In my opinion, McDonald's is not only big business, it's the biggest business there is as far as fast food restaurants are concerned. All sorts of people go there. People who are always in a hurry prefer fast food, because it is so convenient. McDonald's restaurants are open almost around the clock, so it's not surprising that McDonald's make huge profits.

4. "All my friends go to McDonald's, so I go with them, but I don't like it."
   If you don't like fast food restaurants like McDonald's, you should tell your friends. They will not break off their friendship with you which should be based on trust. That's why you have to discuss this problem. I am sure you will find a compromise concerning a suitable restaurant. You need only be a little more self-confident and honest!

5. At McDonald's you can't buy alcoholic drinks with your meal. That makes it a good place for young people.
   Although McDonald's restaurants are interested in making money they do not sell alcoholic drinks. I think that's why these restaurants are better places for young people to go to than others. Besides, teenagers enjoy the relaxed and informal atmosphere. They can afford the meals because they are cheap. As the McDonald's restaurants are open all day and almost all night young people can go there whenever they feel hungry, for example after spending a night at the disco.

6. "Chips! I'm doing the Slimfast diet at the moment. Slimfast and chips is good." (Robbie Williams)
   I think this statement is contradictory. Chips are fatty and salty and make you put on weight. Slimfast is a diet drink and makes you lose weight. So Slimfast and chips combined cannot be good. It can only be unhealthy. It would be very foolish to take Robbie William's statement seriously.

VI. Giving opinion

Useful words and phrases

to be aware of	sich bewusst sein
to be popular with	beliebt bei ...
to be in a hurry	in Eile sein, es ständig eilig haben
to consume	konsumieren
to cause	verursachen
to afford	sich etwas leisten
informal atmosphere	ungezwungene Atmosphäre
to waste time for ...	Zeit verschwenden für ...
variety of meals	Speisenvielfalt

I can partly agree with this statement. In fact, I think fast food is booming but we are not a nation of lazy, unhealthy people.
Fast food is popular with children, teenagers, and all people who are always in a hurry because one saves time. Nowadays, time has become precious in our fast-moving life and that's why fast food has become a part of it. If you have got a job, you are always busy and under stress. You need time for relaxing and forms of recreation. For these reasons most people do not want to waste time on preparing meals every day. Fast food saves time and money that you can spend on activities in your leisure time. I am sure most customers today know about the risks of eating too much fast food. They are aware of the poor quality of those fatty meals. Restaurants and producers have also become aware of this trend and have improved the quality and variety of their meals accordingly. They now also sell seafood, salad, and chicken. Now we have the choice between healthy meals, such as salads and seafood and rather unhealthy meals, such as hamburgers and chips.
By the way, we always have to choose between living healthily or not. Nevertheless, life without fast food would be unthinkable today.

**Realschulabschluss Englisch in Mecklenburg-Vorpommern
Probearbeit 1998**

False Alarm

One day when the sun was shining, Jillian spent her lunch hour sunbathing on the roof of her office building, the BBC House. As it was one of the tallest buildings in the heart of London, she could only dimly hear the noise of the traffic far below. When it was time to go down, however, she could not open the door. She did not want to bang at the door or
5 call for help as it was strictly forbidden to go on the roof, and she was afraid of losing her job.
So she got a piece of paper out of her handbag and wrote a note to her boyfriend Martin, who was working in one of the offices in the building. "I am on the roof. I don't know what to do. Please, help me." She wrote Martin's name and office number on the other side
10 of the note and threw it down into the street, where she saw a man pick it up. He read it, looked up at Jillian and shouted, "Don't worry, I'll see to it." So, seeing him walk away with the letter, Jillian lay down again to sunbathe.
But what she didn't see was the policeman at the corner of the street, who stopped the man with Jillian's letter. "Excuse me, sir," he said, "will you show me that piece of paper?"
15 The policeman read the paper, "I'll look after this." He called the police station telling them a young woman might jump off the BBC House.
His superior told him to stop all traffic immediately, and he called the fire service, an ambulance and all police cars. A police helicopter was called, too. Newspaper reporters and a TV team arrived.
20 In the meantime, the policeman had turned the note round. He at once rushed to Martin's office.
"Will you come with me, please, sir?" the policeman asked.
"Oh, I haven't been breaking the law, have I?" Martin replied.
"No, sir, but will you look at this piece of paper?" the policeman asked.
25 "I think I can handle this. Let me go up alone," Martin suggested. "I must get her down safely. I will get her down safely," he thought.
A minute later he pushed open the roof door, and there was Jillian sunbathing. "Hello, Martin," she greeted him happily. "Look, I've been getting a beautiful tan[1]. Thank you for coming, but I couldn't open that silly door. I say there's a lot of noise down there, isn't
30 there? Now I must go back to my desk. And – er – Martin, you won't tell anybody about this, will you? Or I will lose my job. Cheerio."
Martin was left standing with his mouth wide open.

Quelle: unbekannt

[1] to get a tan: braun werden

Aufgaben

I. Comprehension

1. Matching exercise. Combine the matching parts of the sentences. (6 p.)

   (1) After Jillian had finished her sunbathing on the roof
   (2) She wrote a note on a piece of paper
   (3) A man found it on the street
   (4) The man gave it to a policeman
   (5) Martin went onto the roof
   (6) When he arrived on the roof Martin was very surprised

   a) who thought that Jillian wanted to jump off the BBC House.
   b) because he wanted to get Jillian down safely.
   c) that Jillian was sunbathing there.
   d) and walked away with the paper.
   e) she wasn't able to open the door to get down.
   f) and dropped it onto the street.

   Put the correct letters below the numbers:

(1)	(2)	(3)	(4)	(5)	(6)

2. Read the text carefully. Find out which statements are true and which are false. (9 p.)

   true | false

   a) After she had finished her work Jillian wanted to sunbathe on the roof of the BBC House.
   b) She was not allowed to go onto the roof.
   c) When she wanted to return to the office she could hardly open the door.
   d) She wrote a note to Martin and suggested him to have a sunbath, too.
   e) A man found that note but he was stopped by a policeman.
   f) The policeman told the man to call an ambulance and the fire service.
   g) This policeman had to find Martin in the office, who had the key to the door.
   h) After all Jillian went back to her office alone.
   i) Jillian lost her job.

II. Language

From the 20 words below choose the suitable ones and fill in the gaps. (11 p.)

parents – during – however – prefer – worst – imagine – same – definitely – open – listening – are – easiest – realize – different – producer – because – hearing – while – most – average

Every year the (1) _____ American spends 250 hours (2) _____ to music, 1.500 hours watching TV, 50 hours watching home videos, 95 hours reading books for pleasure, 12 hours watching films. The average German is surely not (3) _____ from the Americans. A lot of people (4) _____ spending their free time in a passive way. They (5) _____ watch too much TV. The TV companies say, "If you don't like it, switch off." But by the time you (6) _____ you don't like it, it's too late. Most people are passive viewers – they don't care what they watch. The (7) _____ problem is the effect on children. They (8) _____ easily influenced by TV (9) _____ they enjoy it and learn to copy violence or crime. The (10) _____ are to be blamed as well as TV. They use television as a cheap babysitter (11) _____ they are going out for a drink.

III. Grammar

1. Fill in the correct words. (8 p.)

noun	verb	adjective
break		
	to open	
		safe
help		

2. Adjective or adverb? Put in the correct forms. (6 p.)

   a) Jillian has a _____ job in an office of the BBC House in London. (good)

   b) She especially liked the _____ place on the roof of the building for sunbathing. (quiet)

   c) But one day when she couldn't open the door to go back to her office, she felt a bit _____. (nervous)

   d) The man on the road _____ gave the note to the policeman. (willing)

   e) At first the policeman didn't read the note _____. (complete)

   f) But then he _____ went to his police car and phoned his superior. (quick)

3. If clauses. Please fill in the correct forms. (3 p.)
   a) If Jillian's boss _____ out where she spent her last lunch hour, he would be very angry with her. (find)
   b) He _____ her job to another young woman if he was a very strict person. (give)
   c) If there is another sunny day, Jillian _____ find a better place for her sunbath during lunch hour. (have to)

4. Passive. Please put the verbs in brackets into the passive voice. (6 p.)
   Here are some bits of information that were published by the BBC.
   a) Blackpool: Last week a press conference _____ (hold) by the Conservative Party in Blackpool.
   b) Oxford: Research shows that English _____ (speak) in more than 86 countries all over the world.
   c) Windsor: Prince Charles _____ (see) in public for the first time since Diana died in a car crash.
   d) Wimbledon: Yesterday Boris Becker _____ (not beat) by Tim Henman.
   e) Berlin: Today the biggest construction site in Europe _____ (find) at the Potsdamer Platz.
   f) Today's weather forecast: Strong winds can _____ (expect), but there'll be sunny skies.

5. Tenses. Please put the verbs in brackets into the correct tense. (8 p.)
   Today Jillian _____ as a secretary. (work)
   She _____ in this office since May. (work)
   Before she _____ this job she _____ a lot of letters of application to various firms. (get; write)
   Now she _____ very glad to be with BBC. (be)
   Her boyfriend _____ a job in this office building, too. (have got)
   They _____ at a Christmas party last year. (meet)
   Next year they _____. (get married)

IV. Using the language in different contexts

Defective dialogue. (18 p.)

After it became known that Jillian had left the roof safely, a reporter is doing some interviews in the street.

Reporter: The police say that the girl was only sunbathing during her lunch break. What do you think about that?

You: _____
_____
_____

Reporter: Are there any leisure activities that y<u>ou</u> are especially fond of?
You: _____

Reporter: The girl might lose her job now. Would you fire her if you were her boss? Why or why not?
You: _____

Reporter: Can you think of any reason why it's forbidden to climb on top of skyscrapers?
You: _____

Reporter: If you had the chance of getting a job in a TV company, would you rather work in the field of music, sport, news, film or documentaries? Give reasons.
You: _____

Reporter: Oh, that's interesting. Now can you please tell our audience who you are and where you come from.
You: _____

(12 contents, 6 correctness)

V. Comment

Comment on *two* of the following statements. Write about 80 words altogether. Count your words. (20 p.)

1. The police can help you always and everywhere.
2. It's good to have a real friend.
3. You shouldn't do anything forbidden.
4. A good friend ignores every mistake.
5. Little lies can sometimes help.

(10 contents, 10 correctness)

VI. Giving opinion

After a long day of hard work everybody is looking forward to a little bit of free time.

Describe *and* discuss the ways people spend their leisure time nowadays. You might think of yourself, your friends, your family ...

Write about 150 words altogether. Count your words. (25 p.)

(15 contents, 10 correctness)

Lösung

I. Comprehension

1.

(1)	(2)	(3)	(4)	(5)	(6)
e	f	d	a	b	c

2. a) false   b) true
   c) false   d) false
   e) true   f) false
   g) false   h) true
   i) false

II. Language

(1) average, (2) listening, (3) different, (4) prefer, (5) definitely, (6) realize, (7) worst, (8) are, (9) because, (10) parents, (11) while

III. Grammar

1.

noun	verb	adjective
break	to break	breakable
opener/opening	to open	open
safety/safe	to save	safe
help	to help	helpful/helpless

2. a) good   b) quiet
   c) nervous   d) willingly
   e) completely   f) quickly

3. a) ... boss **found** out where she ...
   (Hinweis: Nebensatz = Simple Past Typ 2)
   b) He **would give** her job ...
   (Hinweis: Hauptsatz = Would + Infinitive Typ 2)
   c) ..., Jillian **will have to** find ...
   (Hinweis: Hauptsatz = Simple Future Typ 1)

4. Antworten in folgender Reihenfolge
   a) ... a conference **was held** by ...
   (Signalwort = last week, Past Tense)
   b) ... English **is spoken** in ...
   (Allgemeingültige Aussage = Simple Present)

  c) ... Charles **has been seen** in ...
   (Signalwort = since, Simple Present Perfect)
  d) B. Becker **was not beaten** by ...
   (Signalwort = yesterday, Past Tense)
  e) ... in Europe **is found** at ...
   (Allgemeingültige Aussage = Simple Pres.)
  f) ... winds can **be expected,** but ...

5. Antworten in folgender Reihenfolge
 ... Jillian **works** as ...
 (Hinweis: Signalwort = today, Simple Present, allgemeine Aussage)
 She **has worked** in this ...
  (Hinweis: Signalwort = since, Simple Present Perfect)
 ... she **got** this ... she **had written** ...
 (Hinweis: zwei Handlungen liegen in der Vergangenheit, wovon eine im Past Perfect noch vor einer anderen im Simple Past liegt)
 ... she **is** very ...
 (Hinweis: Signalwort = now, Simple Present)
 ... boyfriend **has got** a job ...
 They **met** at a ...
 (Hinweis: Signalwort = last year, Past Tense)
 They **will get married.**
 (Hinweis: Signalwort = next year, Simple Future)

IV. Using the language in different contexts

 You: "I suppose she only wanted to sunbathe. But I think the roof is not a suitable place."
 You: "I enjoy playing basketball and I like reading."
 You: "If I was her boss, I would fire her because it is strictly forbidden to go on the roof."
 You: "In fact, it is very dangerous because one can fall off the roof. But I am sure there are very good reasons for forbidding people to climb onto the roofs of sky-scrapers."
 You: "I would rather work in the field of sport because I am interested in it and I know a lot about sports."
 You: "My name is Martin Häuser and I come from S., a very beautiful town in Mecklenburg Hither Pommerania."

V. Comment

1. The police can help you always and everywhere.
 The crime rate is so high nowadays and the police must work very hard to arrest all the burglars, murderers, robbers and other criminals. Therefore we cannot expect the police to appear immediately whenever and wherever the Law is broken. However if you need their help and call them, they will do their best to help you.

2. It's good to have a real friend.
   To my mind, it is good and very important to have a real friend you can trust and rely on. Sometimes I do not want to discuss my problems with my parents. But I can ask my best friend to help me solve my problems. We support each other and share many interests.

3. You shouldn't do anything forbidden.
   I agree with this statement, although I know that many other young people including my friends think that doing something forbidden is a kind of adventure. In my opinion, there are usually very good reasons for forbidding certain things. Sometimes it is even necessary to forbid something in order to protect people.

4. A good friend ignores every mistake.
   I must contradict this statement. A good friend should be honest and sincere. Therefore he/she can't ignore every mistake. I think he/she should be critical of mistakes in order to help the other person. Ignoring everything does not contribute to a real friendship. I do not ignore the mistakes of my friend.

5. Little lies can sometimes help.
   I can only partly agree with this statement. Little lies are sometimes necessary to avoid disappointing and hurting someone. But there is a limit to everything although it is very difficult to know where to draw the line. Therefore one should avoid lying as much as possible.

VI. Giving opinion

Useful words and phrases

to trust s.b.	jmd. vertrauen
to rely on s.b.	sich auf jmd. verlassen
to help with problems	bei Problemen helfen
to share interests	Interessen teilen
to be critical of mistakes	Fehlern gegenüber kritisch sein
to contribute to	beitragen zu
to avoid sth.	etwas vermeiden
to compensate for	etwas ausgleichen
couch potatoe	Stubenhocker
relaxation	Entspannung
recreation	Erholung
moody	launisch
dissatisfied	unzufrieden
stressful	stressig/anstrengend
exhausted	abgespannt/erschöpft

There are only two ways people can spend their leisure time nowadays: actively or passively.
I prefer the active way of spending my free time because I think it improves the quality of my life. For two years I have been doing a lot of sports. I play volleyball three times a week. In my opinion, sport is healthy and good for you and compensates for stressful work. Therefore I can't understand all those people who spend their leisure time in front of a television set. Television encourages people to be passive.

Unfortunately, my parents also spend most of their free time watching television. They are so exhausted when they come home from work that they only want to relax. For my parents relaxation means doing nothing or watching TV. I am very sad that my mother and father are such "couch potatoes".

But spending leisure time actively doesn't only mean doing sports. I think a proper hobby, apart from watching TV, is also an active way of spending one's free time. My parents are often moody, dissatisfied and terribly bored like many other people who don't participate in some acitvity during their leisure time. Therefore I think, I must help my parents to find suitable activities.

> **Realschulabschluss Englisch in Mecklenburg-Vorpommern**
> **Probearbeit 2000: Listening Comprehension**

You will listen to three different aspects of teenage life

Aufgabe 1: My new room

Hi, Jill. I'm dying to tell you how thrilled I am with my new room. Since we moved into our new house, I've got the best room I've ever had. Really. You must come and see it. I was allowed to decorate it myself and, of course, I painted it pink and put lots of posters of famous teenage actors on the walls. There are also some pictures of me and, yes, the new cuckoo clock my grandmother gave me and two other clocks. I have my own room and my two brothers share a room. It's nice having a room of my own but sometimes I'd like to have someone to talk to at night. I also have a bigger collection of rock CDs now, this is still my favourite kind of music. You see, not everything has changed that much since we've been here in Oxford. In my room I can watch TV or listen to music on my stereo. Nobody disturbs me here. My parents don't mind if I talk on the phone for hours. But my room is also a perfect place for studying. Right after we had moved in, my parents bought me a new writing desk. That's reason enough to work harder for school. When my new classmates come round we often play games on dad's old computer. My bedroom is usually messy, though I do tidy it sometimes. My mum always tells me to use the vacuum cleaner more often because the carpet looks too dirty. But this, like everything else in my room, is my own business

Aufgabe 2: Parents

Welcome everybody here with us on the air. The first part of tonight's programme deals with the problems of parents today. Let's listen to our first interview:
My name is Joe Gray. I have three teenagers, two girls and a boy. I want to tell you it's not easy to have children nowadays. When I was a kid, things were different. my parents never had to worry about drugs and about the dangers for their children on the street. There were some problems with us, but there weren't so many. When I kissed my girlfriend for the first time I was almost 18 years old. I was very excited and didn't know much about sex. Today, when you open a magazine or switch on the TV sex is everywhere. I don't like this. Also drugs and violence weren't around us like they are now. In yesterday's paper I read that very many 15-year-olds smoke regularly, isn't that terrible? A lot of young people drink alcohol at parties and then drive home. Why aren't they more sensible? There are so many accidents because of that. In fact, alcohol is the main reason for road accidents.
Well, I'm a realist. My kids will probably try marijuana and alcohol. These days you can get this stuff everywhere. Of course, I'm against it and I'll try to keep these things away from them, but I know I can't. That's the way it is today. Sometimes I just wish we were back in the good old 1960's again.

Aufgabe 3: Shooting in High School[1]

"I'm standing here right in the middle of lots of excited students at Springfield High School. The school is situated in a quiet and peaceful neighborhood. But this morning something terrible happened. 15-year-old Martin wanted to help his brother, who was fighting with another boy. He tried to stop him from hitting his brother and so he pulled a gun. He wanted to fire a warning shot but by mistake he killed another student, Jake Hall, who was just walking there. That was a big shock for everybody including Martin himself.
Here with me is Martin's history teacher. She's just told me that Martin has always been such a friendly person. Like other teachers she's sure that Martin didn't really want to hurt anyone.

Why are fights on the schoolyard increasing? What makes young people so violent nowadays? Many schools say it's because of the activities of teenage gangs who bring violence from the streets into the schools. It's so easy to buy a gun these days. That's why students like Martin cannot imagine how dangerous they can be.
Some people say that there is just a small number of really violent kids and that they need stricter discipline. I'm sure this will also have to be discussed in this neighborhood."

1 This text is written in American English

Aufgabe 1: My new room (6 p)
On the phone Ann describes her room to her friend in York. Listen to her phone-call and tick ☑ what she said.

1. In her new room Ann has
   posters of
   - ☐ a pink colour.
   - ☐ famous walls.
   - ☐ teenage actors.

2. Ann's grandma gave her
   - ☐ a new cuckoo clock.
   - ☐ an old cuckoo clock.
   - ☐ two other clocks.

3. Ann has
   - ☐ one brother.
   - ☐ one sister.
   - ☐ two brothers.

4. Ann's new house is in
   - ☐ Oxford.
   - ☐ London.
   - ☐ York.

5. In Ann's room you don't find
   - ☐ a new writing desk.
   - ☐ a new computer.
   - ☐ a TV-set.

6. Ann doesn't
   - ☐ use the vacuum cleaner very often.
   - ☐ tidy her room.
   - ☐ like her mum.

Aufgabe 2: Parents
Tonight's radio programme deals with parents' opinions on young people today. Listen carefully to what one father has to say. Try to find out if the following information is true or false. ☑ (7 p)

	true	false
1. John Gray is a father of three youngsters.	☐	☐
2. His parents had no problems with their children.	☐	☐
3. He was older than 18 when he kissed his girlfriend for the first time.	☐	☐
4. John Gray doesn't like sex in the media.	☐	☐
5. Many young people drink and drive.	☐	☐
6. Gray's kids will never try marijuana.	☐	☐
7. He liked the 1960s.	☐	☐

Aufgabe 3: Shooting in High School![1]

During the last few years the media were full of reports on teenage violence in schools. Listen to our 'On The Spot' reporter Gary Brown with the latest sad news from Springfield High School.. There have been some errors during broadcasting. Underline and correct them. (7 p)

1. "I'm standing here right in the middle of lots of excited students at

2. Springfield High School. The school is situated in a quiet and peaceful

3. neighborhood. But this afternoon something terrible happened.

4. 15-year-old Martin wanted to help his brother, who was fighting with

5. another boy. He tried to stop him from hurting his brother and so he pulled

6. a gun. He wanted to fire a warning shot but by mistake he killed another

7. student, Jake Hall, who was just working there. That was a big shock for

8. everybody including Martin himself. Here with me is Martin's history

9. teacher. She's just told me that Martin has always been such a friendly

10. person. Like other teachers she's sure that Martin didn't really mean to

11. hurt anyone. Why are fights on the schoolyard increasing? What makes

12. young pupils so violent nowadays? Many schools say it's because of the

13. activities of teenage gangs who bring violence from the streets into

14. the schools. It's so easy to sell a gun these days. That's why students

A 4

15. like Martin cannot imagine how dangerous they can be.

16. Some people say that there is only a small number of really violent kids

17. and that they need stricter discipline. I'm sure this will also have to be

18. discussed in this neighborhood."

Lösung

Aufgabe 1

1 teenage actors
2 a new cuckoo clock
3 two brothers
4 Oxford
5 a new computer
6 use the vacuum cleaner very often

Aufgabe 2

1 t, 2 f, 3 f, 4 t, 5 t, 6 f, 7 t

Aufgabe 3

	falsch	richtig
Zeile 3	afternoon	morning
Zeile 5	hurting	hitting
Zeile 7	working	walking
Zeile 10	mean	want
Zeile 12	pupils	people
Zeile 14	sell	buy
Zeile 16	only	just

Bullying

Nobody expects school to be fun all the time. Nervous teachers, too much work and boring lessons can all make life miserable for pupils. But for some young people, school is more than just miserable, it can be hell. Victims of bullying and other school violence are so frightened that they become seriously ill or start playing truant[1].

5 Rebecca, now 16, told a reporter from *The Guardian* about her bad experiences at school. "At first they only called me names but then they started doing other things like locking me in class or slamming doors in my face. It became so bad that I didn't want to go to school any longer and I just stopped eating because I felt so sad. I had to spend four months in hospital because I was starving." Doctors said her illness was a result of the
10 stress caused by bullying.

Mark, 12, remembered his moving to another school last September. "There's quite a lot of bullying at school. I got bullied because I was a new boy. Where we catch the bus there's a subway you have to go under and all these bigger boys stood there throwing stones and calling me names. I felt horrible."

15 Pupils at school are bullied for many different reasons. Because they are too tall – or too fat – or too thin. Because they aren't good at sports. Because people don't like their clothes. Bullying can be a very painful and emotional experience for the victim. Every year around ten young people in Britain commit suicide because they are victims of bullying.

20 Steve, 16, was often beaten up as a young teenager. "My brother said, 'You must give them something back.' So I did. I started fighting back and became hard. When you hit them it makes you feel great. I love it. The girls encourage you. They like to be with the hard people. You hit people because you want to show off – prove yourself. I was the hardest at school. When you hit someone they remember you. You ask them to give you
25 money and they do, yeah. When you've hit them, they'll do whatever you say. Sometimes they cry and that makes you feel really good. – Life at home is boring," explained Steve. "My parents stopped my pocket money to punish my bad behaviour, they said. But without money you don't get what you need …"

There are many different forms of bullying. Rowdy kids interrupt the lessons and this is
30 bad for pupils who want to learn. They hurt and threaten other teenagers, steal their money, blackmail them, kick them and even hit them brutally. They don't really get enough punishment for what they do at school. Often those bullies even say everything was just fun and usually they don't realize they are doing wrong.

---

1 to play truant: die Schule schwänzen

Aufgaben

I. Comprehension

1. Matching exercise. Combine the matching parts of the sentences: (6 p.)

   (1) Bullying can make
   (2) Rebecca ended up in hospital
   (3) A boy got bullied
   (4) Bullying at school can even lead
   (5) Unfortunately some girls
   (6) Threatening other teenagers, interrupting lessons or stealing

   a) are only some forms of bullying.
   b) support bullying at school.
   c) because of her bad experiences at school.
   d) a lot of pupils sick.
   e) to suicide.
   f) because he was a new pupil.

(1)	(2)	(3)	(4)	(5)	(6)

2. Read the text carefully. Find out which statements are true and which are false. Mark with a cross. (8 p.)

   true | false

   1. For some pupils school is extremely hard because they are victims of bullying.
   2. Rebecca is a reporter from *The Guardian* who writes an article about violence at school.
   3. A sixteen-year-old girl stopped eating because she was too fat.
   4. Last September Mark changed school.
   5. Clothes are one of many reasons for bullying.
   6. When Steve was younger, he was a victim of bullying, too.
   7. Steve didn't get any pocket money from his parents because he had bad marks at school.
   8. Steve is pleased when his victims cry.

II. Language

From the words below choose the suitable ones and fill in the gaps. (11 p.)

seriously – problems – secondary – violent – at – suffered – punishment – kind – friendly – discuss – part – have – anyone – out – get

A recent survey in Britain found that three-quarters of all (1) _____ school students have been bullies and a similar number have been victims (2) _____ least once a year. Victims of bullying often find it hard to (3) _____ help.

No boy who took (4) _____ in the survey had contacted a telephone bullying helpline.

Almost 80 per cent of the pupils said that they told their parents about their (5) _____. But 10 per cent did not report the attack to (6) _____.

That's why many English schools (7) _____ an anti-bullying programme.

At some schools there is a (8) _____ of "Bullying Court"[2] which is operated by the pupils themselves. The aggressive and (9) _____ behaviour of the offenders is brought before this court. Otherwise everything goes on unnoticed.

The pupils also (10) _____ with their teachers some form of (11) _____ for the bully. In this way bullies are tried by their own peers.

2 court: Gericht

III. Grammar

1. Fill in the correct words. (8 p.)

noun	verb	adjective
		punishable
	to differ	
acceptance		
		supportive

2. Adjective – Comparison: Put in the correct forms (8 p.)

Bob moved to Somerton last year. He was quite _____ (unhappy) when he had to leave his football team and his friends.

Although Bob is very small he was the _____ (fast) player on his team.

Of course, he kept in touch with Tim, who is not as _____ (skilful) as Bob but the _____ (good) friend he's ever had.

As the boys don't have much time together anymore, they write _____ (many) e-mails than ever before. In the beginning Bob also wrote about his new situation in Somerton.

The first days at his new school were the _____ (difficult) of his life. He got bullied because of his height: Bob is _____ (small) than anybody else in his class.

They started to call him names, and other pupils pushed him. However, Bob didn't get frightened. He talked to others and found support. Together they feel _____ (strong) now than the bullies.

3. If clauses. Please fill in the correct forms. (3 p.)
   a) Teachers could help their pupils against the bullies if they _____ (know) about their activities.
   b) Some youngsters _____ (have) fewer problems if they had real friends to talk to.
   c) If you _____ (not find) someone you can trust, you will feel left alone with your problems.

4. Questions (5 p.)
   Finally in hospital, Rebecca is telling her story. Try to get more information by asking questions.
   a) "One day I stopped eating."
      Why _____?
   b) "That was because my classmate bullied me."
      Who _____?
   c) "I've already been in hospital for a long time."
      How long exactly _____?
   d) "Dr Bradley helps me a lot."
      In which way _____?
   e) "I'll change school."
      When _____?

5. Tenses. Please put the verbs in brackets into the correct tense. (8 p.)

   Maria and Tony _____ (know) each other for three months. Tony is two years older than Maria, but they still go to the same high school.

   Tony _____ (play) football every Friday evening and he wants Maria to watch him.

   So last week Maria _____ (give up) her dancing to please him.

   Tony _____ (go) to college next September.

   Yesterday he gave Maria a ring and _____ (tell) her not to date anyone but him. Since then Maria _____ (lose) her freedom.

   In general, Maria really likes Tony, but sometimes he scares her because he _____ (be) so jealous and dominant.

   She isn't sure anymore what _____ (become) of such a pressure in the future.

IV. Using the language in different contexts

Defective dialogue: Questionnaire (18 p.)

In order to get some more information on the topic of violence among young people in Europe, *The Guardian* has sent out questionnaires. Here is one for you to fill in. **Write about 80 words altogether.**

What kind of people would you call "cool"?

_____
_____

How would you describe the relationship among the pupils in your class?

_____
_____

Which role does violence play at your school?

_____
_____

What do you think of violence in films like *Star Wars?*

_____
_____

In your opinion, what are the most common reasons for bullying?

_____
_____

Suggest what should be changed at your school. Please give examples.

_____
_____
_____

V. Comment/Giving opinion

Write down your opinion on **one or two** of the following statements. (25 p.)

Give reasons for your opinion and/or examples. Write about 150 words altogether. Count your words.

- Violence on TV should be banned.
- There are situations in which you need good friends.
- Strict punishment for hooligans!
- Pocket money is essential for youngsters.
- Young people have many things to worry about.

Lösung

I. Comprehension

1.

(1)	(2)	(3)	(4)	(5)	(6)
d	c	f	e	b	a

2. 1) true   2) false
   3) false   4) true
   5) true   6) true
   7) false   8) true

II. Language

(1) secondary, (2) at, (3) get, (4) part, (5) problems, (6) anyone, (7) have, (8) kind, (9) violent, (10) discuss, (11) punishment

III. Grammar

1.

noun	verb	adjective
punishment	to punish	punishable
difference	to differ	different
acceptance	to accept	acceptable
supporter	to support	supportive

2. a) unhappy   b) fastest
   c) skilful   d) best
   e) more   f) most difficult
   g) smaller   h) stronger

3. … if they **knew** about their activities.
   (Hinweis: HS = could + Infinitive = NS = Simple Past)
   … youngsters **would have** fewer problems …
   (Hinweis: NS = Simple Past = HS = would + Infinitive)
   If you **don't find** someone …
   (Hinweis: HS = Simple Future = NS = Simple Present)

4. a) Why **did you stop eating?**
   b) Who **bullied you/was that/did that?**
   c) How long exactly **have you been in hospital/here?**
   d) In which way **does Dr Bradley/he/she help you?**
   e) When **will you change school?**

5. Antworten in folgender Reihenfolge

   ... and Tony **have known** each other ...
   (Hinweis: Signalwort = for three months, Simple Present Perfect)

   Tony **plays** football ...
   (Hinweis: Signalwort = every Friday, Simple Present)

   ... Maria **gave up** her dancing ...
   (Hinweis: Signalwort = last week, Simple Past)

   Tony **will go** to college ...
   (Hinweis: Signalwort = next September, Simple Future)

   ... a ring and **told** her not to ...
   (Hinweis: Signalwort = yesterday, Simple Past)

   ... Maria **has lost** her freedom.
   (Hinweis: Signalwort = since then, Simple Present Perfect)

   ... because he **is** so jealous ...
   (Hinweis: Signalwort = sometimes, Simple Present)

   ... what **will become** of such ...
   (Hinweis: Signalwort = in the future, Simple Future)

IV. Using the language in different contexts

You: "I think "cool" is a negative word describing people who don't care about other people's opinions and feelings."

You: "I like my classmates because they are almost all very helpful and friendly. Therefore the relationship among the pupils in my class is good."

You: "It is sad but there are pupils at my school who are not able to discuss problems. They are often very argumentative and aggressive, which sometimes leads to fights."

You: "Violence seems to be normal in films like *Star Wars* but in my opinion cruel and violent scenes are not necessary to make a film exciting."

You: "It is difficult to say. But I think the most common reasons for bullying are aggression and drive for personal prestige."

You: "I would say that the teachers should use special lessons more intensively for learning to handle conflicts pupils have with each other. Or we could organize project lessons."

V. Comment / Giving opinion

- **Violence on TV should be banned.**

  I agree with this statement although I am not convinced that this alone is the solution to the problem. To my mind, it is difficult to say whether there is a connection between violence on TV and in real life. But I think that too many violent programmes are broadcast at times when youngsters usually watch TV. Cartoons or science fiction films are sometimes full of violent scenes. Children and teenagers are easily influenced and take movie heroes as an example. They often think there is no difference between TV and real life and that violence is normal. Therefore I think violent programmes should not be completely banned from TV but should be broadcast at times when youngsters do not usually watch TV.

- **There are situations in which you need good friends.**

  Although I owe a very loving upbringing to my mother and father I think there are sometimes situations in which I am very happy to have a good friend. Therefore I fully agree with this statement.

  I have chosen my friend quite carefully and I can trust her and rely on her. I especially do not want to discuss problems with boys with my parents. Some weeks ago I broke up with my boyfriend. My friend Sabine was not only a great comfort to me, she also gave me advice. Therefore I think it is very important to have a good friend who stands by you.

- **Strict punishment for hooligans!**

  The recent incidents during the European Soccer Championships determined my opinion that it is necessary to punish hooligans for their violent riots, so I fully agree with this statement.

  What have brutal fights between so-called fans got to do with soccer? It is a shame and frustrating for a real soccer fan that the sport is not the centre of attention anymore but the brutal attacks of hooligans. Therefore I think it is of great importance to take sanctions against them.

- **Pocket money is essential for youngsters.**

  There are a large variety of leisure and entertainment facilities for young people. Theatres, concerts and cinemas attract youngsters to do things which are not free of charge. Quite the contrary! Tickets for all events are often very expensive. Therefore I think pocket money is essential for youngsters. Parents should take care to give their children an appropriate amount of money regularly.

  In my opinion, pocket money is a good opportunity for teaching youngsters to spend money carefully.

- **Young people have many things to worry about.**

  In my opinion it is a hard fact that we young people do not only enjoy our lives but also have a lot of problems. Therefore I would say this statement is true.

  I do not think it is easy for us to find out which job might be the right one and it is becoming more and more difficult to get an apprenticeship. Another thing we worry about is the growing pollution and destruction of our environment. A lot of damage has already been done to human health and nature. There are too many careless people about.

  Young people are also afraid of the upward tendency of violence and aggression in everyday life. Finally, I think our youth is far from being a time without conflicts and worries but I am convinced it is a happy time as well.

Useful words and phrases
to ban s.th.	–	etwas verbieten
to punish s.b.	–	jmd. bestrafen
to take sanctions against	–	gegen jmd. Strafen verhängen
to be a comfort to s.b.	–	jmd. Trost sein
to pay attention to s.th.	–	auf etwas achten
upward tendency	–	steigende Tendenz
appropriate amount	–	angemessener Betrag

Realschulabschluss Englisch in Mecklenburg-Vorpommern
Abschlussprüfung 1996

Terry

Terry lived with his parents and younger sister in a quiet village. He enjoyed living in the country, where he worked in a small printing firm.
"A quiet boy who works well," his last school report said. His sister Jill, a year younger and still at school, was the lively one in the family, always surrounded by friends and a
5 popular figure at school. Terry stayed at home many evenings, and often helped his father in their large garden. He even helped his sister with her homework.
His favourite hobby was fishing, which he enjoyed with several of his old school friends.
Every Friday evening he and his friends went to the Youth Club meeting at the village hall. It was a chance to meet more old friends, and he enjoyed being in the large group,
10 sharing the general talk and laughter, the music and whistling at the girls.
Terry did not dance and none of his group was very interested in girls. He had never enjoyed the company of those boys at school who could talk of nothing else and bragged about their adventures with girls to everyone.
One weekend his sister brought a group of her friends to tea, as she did quite often. Terry
15 wanted to keep out of their way, as he usually did, but he noticed a newcomer, a girl whose family had moved into the district a few weeks ago. Her name, he soon learned, was Mollie.
He spent most of the afternoon hanging around hoping to see her again. Then, by chance, he almost bumped into her as the girls came out into the garden. She smiled and said hello.
20 They started to talk and he had just begun to describe the Youth Club evenings when his sister called her. "Maybe I'll see you there one day," said Mollie as she left. She was smiling, and Terry thought he had never seen such a warm, attractive smile.
The following days Terry could not forget the girl – he had never felt like this before. Finally he asked his sister to get to know more about Mollie.
25 Friday evening came at last. Mollie would not come, he told himself, her parents would not allow it. But suddenly she entered with another girl. Awkwardly he found a table for the three of them and bought drinks. It was so difficult to start a
30 sensible conversation. Perhaps it would be better to just sit and listen to the records for a while. Suddenly Mollie said, "Do you dance?"
Terry's heart sank. "Not really," he said
35 in a low voice. It seemed as if everyone in the hall was staring at him.
At that moment Alf, one of the motor-bike gang, came boldly to the table and faced Mollie. "Have a dance, love?" he
40 grinned.
Mollie smiled. "Thank you," she said, "but I'm Terry's guest this evening."

Aufgaben

I. Comprehension

1. Matching exercise. Combine the matching parts of the sentences: (6 p.)

   (1) Terry often helped
   (2) In his spare time he liked
   (3) Terry always looked forward to Friday evenings
   (4) This weekend was especially exciting for him
   (5) Terry hoped
   (6) It wasn't easy for him to start a conversation

   a) because he met his old school friends in the Youth Club.
   b) to get to know her better.
   c) because he saw a new girl with an attractive smile.
   d) because he was a shy boy.
   e) his father and his sister with their work.
   f) to go fishing with his friends.

   Put the correct letters below the numbers:

(1)	(2)	(3)	(4)	(5)	(6)

2. Read the text carefully. Find out which statements are true and which are false. (8 p.)

true	false	
		a) Terry didn't like living in the quiet village.
		b) He was a quiet boy but his sister was very lively.
		c) Terry only sometimes went into the Youth Club because he was so shy.
		d) Mollie was smiling at him when she said she might see him at the club one day.
		e) Friday evening came but Terry did not meet Mollie in the club.
		f) Dancing was one of Terry's favourite hobbies.
		g) Mollie's parents didn't allow her to go to the Youth Club.
		h) Mollie refused when another boy wanted to dance with her.

II. Language

From the 20 words below choose the suitable ones and fill in the gaps. (10 p.)

asked – village – feelings – although – meeting – sad – like – in fact – happy – fun – city – remembered – had fallen in love – simple – event – invited – attractive – admired – believe – lively

A lot of young people (1) _____ living in big cities because there are more facilities for them than in the country. But Terry enjoyed living in his small (2) _____ together with his parents and his younger sister Jill.

The Youth Club meeting every Friday was always a special (3) _____. It was a chance for Terry to meet his old friends. They had a lot of (4) _____. Terry's sister was a very (5) _____ girl and she often (6) _____ her friends to tea. (7) _____ Terry tried to keep out of their way, he noticed a new, attractive girl, called Mollie. Over the following days Terry realized that he (8) _____ with her. Terry couldn't (9) _____ that Mollie would come to the Youth Club on Friday. When she entered the room Terry felt very (10) _____.

III. Grammar

1. Fill in the correct words. (6 p.)

noun	verb	adjective
		lively
	to hope	
attraction		

2. Adjective or adverb? Put in the right form. (5 p.)
    a) Terry was a very _____ boy. (helpful)
    b) He stayed at home very often and helped his family _____. (willing)
    c) Terry couldn't dance _____. (good)
    d) Mollie was a friendly girl and very _____. (attractive)
    e) When Terry saw Mollie enter the room he _____ looked for a table and bought some drinks. (excited)

3. Comparison. Fill in the correct forms. (6 p.)

	comparative	superlative
nice		
	worse	
		most difficult

4. Reported speech (8 p.)

    Please report what Jill said about her brother Terry.

    "Terry is a quiet and friendly boy. He often helped me willingly. It's a pity that he hasn't found a nice girlfriend yet. But it seems that he likes Mollie. Perhaps he will meet her at the Youth Club again."

Jill told one of her friends that Terry ...

_____
_____
_____
_____
_____
_____
_____
_____

5. Please put the verbs in brackets into the correct tense. (8 p.)

I _____ (live) with my parents and my sister in this village for some years. Last year I _____ (leave) school and _____ (find) work in a small printing firm. Every Friday I _____ (meet) all my friends at the Youth Club at the village hall. Next Saturday I _____ (go fishing) with my best friends because it's our hobby. My sister always _____ (invite) her friends to tea. Last week she _____ (bring) a new girl I _____ never _____ (see) before.

IV. Using the language in different contexts

Defective dialogue (15 p.)

It's Saturday afternoon. Terry is just leaving his house when Jim, one of his friends, comes through the front gate.

Jim: "Hi, Terry. Good to see you. Are you going out?"
Terry: _____
_____
_____

Jim: "Oh, yeah, I saw you talking and even dancing with her last night. I had never seen you dance before ..."
Terry: _____
_____
_____

Jim: "Tell me how you met her."
Terry: _____
_____
_____

Jim: "She must be someone special. What makes her different from the others?"
Terry: _____
_____

Jim: "Really? Alf asked her to dance and she said 'no' ... I can't believe it. Tell me more about it!"

Terry: _____
_____
_____

Jim: "Lucky you! OK, I'll better go then. Have a nice afternoon with Mollie."

V. Comment

Comment on *two* of the following statements. Write about 10 sentences altogether. (20 p.)

1. One can only feel sorry for Terry.
2. It's not only fine feathers that make fine birds.[1]
3. Love is more important than anything else.
4. It's very difficult to make friends.
5. Living in the country is awfully boring.
6. It's very important to have hobbies in your leisure time.

_____
_____
_____
_____
_____

(10 contents, 10 correctness)
1 Poolpunkt

[1] etwa: "Kleider machen Leute"

VI. Giving opinion

You meet a lot of people every day. Explain why you choose some people to be your friends but not others (think of clothes, money, humour, hobbies, opinions, attitudes, age ...). Describe the qualities an ideal girlfriend /boyfriend should have and try to give reasons for your opinion. Write about 100 words. (25 p.)

_____
_____
_____
_____
_____
_____

(15 contents, 10 correctness)
2 Poolpunkte

Lösung

I. Comprehension

1.

(1)	(2)	(3)	(4)	(5)	(6)
e	f	a	c	b	d

2. a) false   b) true
   c) false   d) true
   e) false   f) false
   g) false   h) true

II. Language

(1) like, (2) village, (3) event, (4) fun, (5) lively, (6) invited, (7) Although, (8) had fallen in love, (9) believe, (10) happy

III. Grammar

1.

noun	verb	adjective
life	**to live**	lively
hope	to hope	**hopeful**
attraction	**to attract**	attractive

2. a) helpful   b) willingly
   c) well   d) attractive
   e) excitedly

3.

	comparative	superlative
nice	**nicer**	**nicest**
bad	worse	**worst**
difficult	**more difficult**	most difficult

4. Antworten in folgender Reihenfolge

   Terry **was** a quiet and friendly boy.
   He **had** often **helped** her willingly.
   It **was** a pity that he **hadn't found** a nice girl yet.
   But it **seemed** that he **liked** Mollie.
   Perhaps he **would meet** her at the Youth Club again.

5. Gap text: tenses: Antworten in folgender Reihenfolge

have lived/have been living
(Hinweis: Signalwort = for, Simple Present Perfect bzw. Present Perfect Progressive)
left
(Hinweis: Signalwort = last year, Simple Past)
found
(Hinweis: Simple Past)
meet
(Hinweis: Signalwort = every day, Simple Present)
will go fishing
(Hinweis: Signalwort = next Saturday, Simple Future)

IV. Defective dialogue

Mögliche Antworten können z. B. sein:
Terry: "Hello Jim. Yes I am. I am meeting Mollie."
Terry: "That's true, but I couldn't say 'no'."
Terry: "Well I met her at home together with Jill's other friends."
Terry: "Oh, she has got this attractive smile and she refused to dance with Alf."
Terry: "Alf walked up to our table and asked Mollie for a dance. But Mollie told him she was my guest and wouldn't dance with him."

V. Comment

1. One can feel sorry for Terry.
   To my mind, this statement is wrong. One need not feel sorry for Terry. He is in contrast to other boys very shy and sometimes awkward and he has not been interested in girls so far. However Terry is a modest and polite young man who impressed Mollie by his amiable manner. I am sure Terry will go out with Mollie and that's why one may well be envious of Terry instead.

2. It's not only fine feathers that make fine birds.
   It is a sad fact that young people attach more and more importance to clothes, especially to clothes with brand names. Therefore I fully agree with this saying. The personality of a person is more important than the clothes he or she wears. Unfortunately people are very much influenced in their judgement by such superficial things as clothes.

3. Love is more important than anything else.
   Without doubt love is fundamental to happiness. Without love we cannot start a family and educate our children. When we consider the problems all over the world we will realize that there isn't enough love about. Therefore I agree with this statement and would add that such attributes as trust, respect and honesty can only exist where there is love.

4. It's very difficult to make friends.
   In fact, it becomes more and more difficult to make real friends. I know a lot of young people who do not realize what friendship means. In my opinion, trust and honesty serve as a basis for a good friendship as well as common interests. Every day you

have many opportunities to meet people. However it takes time to find out whether a person is a real friend.

5. Living in the country is awfully boring.
It depends on the interests people have. Living in the country can be very boring for those who need a large variety of entertainment facilities like cinemas, theatres, concerts and museums. But if you enjoy walking, jogging and cycling, living in the country is really interesting and not at all boring.

6. It's very important to have hobbies in your leisure time.
I am convinced that it is very important to have hobbies in order to spend one's leisure time properly. Pursuing interesting hobbies makes you feel satisfied and happy. Whether sport, music, or needlework; interesting activities help you to develop your personality. Furthermore you are less likely to get involved with drugs or alcohol if you pursue an interesting and sensible hobby..

VI. Giving opinion

Useful words and phrases

to attach great importance to	großen Wert legen auf
to depend on	abhängen von
to choose	auswählen
to realize	begreifen
to be based	basiert auf
to pursue a hobby	ein Hobby betreiben
leisure/free time	Freizeit
clothes and appearance	Kleidung und Aussehen
personality	Persönlichkeit
trust/to trust	das Vertrauen/jmd. trauen
relationship	Beziehung/Partnerschaft
modest	bescheiden
honest	ehrlich
polite	höflich
cheerful	fröhlich
patient	geduldig
helpful	hilfsbereit
sincere	aufrichtig
shy	schüchtern

I am 16 years old and I attend a school with about 570 students. In my leisure time I play volleyball in a popular team of my hometown, so I meet a lot of people every day. But only a few of them I call friends. I have chosen my friends very carefully. Firstly, I do not attach great importance to the appearance, clothes, and property of a person. Character traits and manners are more important to me.
My ideal girlfriend/boyfriend should be honest and sincere because I think trust serves as a basis for a good friendship. I also want to be able to rely on her/him therefore she/he must be reliable. Furthermore, we should share some interests. Finally, I think an ideal girlfriend/boyfriend must be critical of my faults because a friendship should make a contribution to the development of my personality. Nowadays it is not easy to make real friends, but I think a good friendship improves the quality of life.

**Realschulabschluss Englisch in Mecklenburg-Vorpommern
Abschlussprüfung 1997**

Ecstasy

At first, the party on Saturday, November 11 went well. Mrs Betts said that "no one was drunk, no one was high". Then, soon after midnight, Leah collapsed. Before she went into a coma, she told her father, Paul Betts, 49, that she had bought an Ecstasy tablet. Leah later died in hospital. The tragic death of Leah Betts, a typical "nice" young girl from a
5 *good home, who knew all about the risks, shows how hard it is to convince young people that Ecstasy is dangerous. Many parents will now worry even more when their teenage children go out to parties and clubs.*

IT IS midnight at a club in London. Lights flash, loud techno music plays. Young people dance wildly. Outside, there is a poster banning the use of Ecstasy. But most of the teen-
10 agers inside have taken the drug, despite all the warnings about its dangers.
For many teenagers, going to a rave means taking 'E'. Those who use it say it makes them feel optimistic and warm about everything and everyone they see. One teen described it like this: "You don't feel cold, you don't feel pain. Everything is beautiful and you can dance all night."
15 Ecstasy is taken by an estimated 5 million young people in Britain. The so-called "love-drug" started off in the United States, where it was used by rich Yuppies[1] as an expensive way of getting high. It was banned in the U.S. in 1985, but kids on the other side of the Atlantic then began taking it. For the 15–25 age group, Ecstasy is now Europe's most popular drug after cannabis.
20 Like all dope, Ecstasy can be very dangerous. Over the past five years, more than 50 addicts[2] have died of dehydration[3] after taking Ecstasy. The youngest victim of 'E' was 16, the oldest 24.
Ecstasy may also have longterm effects. Doctors fear that it could cause serious depression years later.
25 Most young people know about at least some of these risks. Just like alcohol and smoking, 'E' is not only dangerous but also pleasurable and people just ignore the risks and concentrate on the fun. They play down the experts' warnings.
A *Newsweek*[4] reporter talked to young people at a London club where Ecstasy is often used. The girls and their friends said, Ecstasy was a "door into a perfect world where every-
30 one loves each other and dreams come true".
Young people think Ecstasy is an acceptable, fashionable drug, unlike hard drugs such as heroin or cocaine. It is taken by young people in clubs, as well as by bankers, lawyers, office workers – even those who really should know better, like medical students.
Ecstasy is expensive, too. One tablet costs from £ 10 to £ 15.

Quelle: READ ON 2/96, Eilers und Schünemann Verlag. Bremen

1 Yuppies: young business people
2 addict: Süchtiger, Abhängiger
3 dehydration: Wasserverlust
4 Newsweek: American magazine

Aufgaben

I. Comprehension

1. Matching exercise. Combine the matching parts of the sentences. (6 p.)

   (1) Ecstasy is called
   (2) A lot of teenagers take 'E'
   (3) First, it was taken
   (4) Despite all warnings
   (5) People who take 'E'
   (6) Young people at a London club said that Ecstasy

   a) by rich Yuppies in the USA.
   b) was a door into a perfect world.
   c) when they are at a party.
   d) may get depressions later on.
   e) "love drug".
   f) young people ignore the dangers.

   Put the correct letters below the numbers.

(1)	(2)	(3)	(4)	(5)	(6)

2. Read the text carefully. Find out which statements are true and which are false. Mark with a cross. (8 p.)

true	false	
		a) Leah took 'E' although she knew about its risks.
		b) In America everybody could afford buying Ecstasy.
		c) It started off in Asian countries.
		d) In the seventies it was banned in the USA.
		e) Ecstasy became popular in Europe about 25 years ago.
		f) In Europe young people still prefer cannabis to Ecstasy.
		g) People take Ecstasy because it makes them feel great.
		h) Medical students don't take Ecstasy.

II. Language

From the 20 words below choose the suitable ones and fill in the gaps. (11 p.)

woke up – expensive – unconscious – popular – tablet – tragic – banned – courage – trouble – fashion – agreed – pleasurable – celebrate – schoolgirl – hoped – ignore – sad – risky – cared – advises

Leah Betts had everything she needed. The Essex (1) _____ was studying for her A levels and (2) _____ to become a teacher. But first, she wanted to (3) _____ her 18th birthday in style with a big party. Her parents (4) _____, and her father even stayed at home to make sure there was no drug-taking or (5) _____ at the party. Her father is a retired police inspector, and her stepmother, Janet, is a nurse who (6) _____ schoolchildren against taking drugs. They (7) _____ a lot

97-2

about their daughter. While Leah was still in hospital, alive, but (8) _____, police began investigations to find out who had given her the (9) _____ she had taken. Like Leah's parents they were (10) _____ and shocked.

At her grave the priest asked all young people to find the (11) _____ to say 'no' to drugs.

III. Grammar

1. Fill in the correct words. (8 p.)

noun	verb	adjective
		pleasurable
	to hope	
depression		
		risky

2. Adjective or adverb? Put in the correct forms. (5 p.)

   a) At midnight you can hear the disco music playing _____.
      (loud)
   b) It is _____ to try drugs at a rave.
      (fashionable)
   c) After taking 'E', Leah felt _____.
      (happy)
   d) Leah's friends were _____ upset when she collapsed.
      (terrible)
   e) Although her parents took her to hospital _____, she died.
      (quick)

3. If clauses. Please fill in the correct forms. (3 p.)

   a) If 'E' is banned, less young people _____. (die)
   b) People wouldn't take the drug so easily if it _____ them feel good.
      (not make)
   c) If 'E' was more expensive, fewer youngsters _____ it.
      (take)

4. Reported speech (8 p.)

   Please report what Louise said at the disco.

   "Ecstasy makes me feel optimistic. Suddenly you are in a perfect world where everyone loves each other. I've never felt like this before. It was absolutely fantastic. People won't stop taking 'E'."

   Louise said that ...

   _____
   _____

5. Tenses. Please put the verbs in brackets into the correct tense. (8 p.)

Only 2 months _____ (pass) since Leah's death and there is a new tragic case in Britain.
The latest victim of 'E', 19-year-old Andy Bouzis, _____ (die) last January. He often _____ (go) to rave parties and he always wanted to _____ (have) fun.
But his mother _____ (tell) Scotland Yard yesterday that she was sure he _____ never _____ (take) any drugs before.
"Now he _____ (be) dead," she said. "But I hope this _____ (keep) other youngsters from taking the drug in future."

IV. Using the language in different contexts

Defective dialogue. (18 p.)

It's Friday night at a fashionable disco. Andy, Louise and their friends are having fun on the dance-floor.

Andy: "Hey, Louise, I'm not in good form tonight. I'm too slow."
Louise: _____

Andy: "That's not true. I can't move in time with the beat."
Louise: _____

Andy: "What do you mean by 'dope'? Do you think I should take hard stuff?"
Louise: _____

Andy: "Try Ecstasy? But that's dangerous, too. Haven't you heard of Leah Betts?"
Louise: _____

Andy: "So you tell me, if I drink enough, nothing bad will happen to me?"
Louise: _____

Andy: "Well, I'm not taking any risk, even if it's 'tiny' as you call it. I better sit down and have a break. A slow dance with you is better than a fast one with death."

(12 contents, 6 correctness)

V. Comment

Comment on *two* of the following statements. Write about 80 words altogether. Count your words. (20 p.)

1. I think there are not many youngsters taking drugs in our country.
2. Ecstasy is dangerous for young people's lives.
3. Drugs are necessary if you want to have fun at a party.
4. Parents should teach their children how to handle alcohol.
5. Schools and teenage magazines don't give enough information on drugs.
6. 'E' kills fewer people than peanuts or sweets.
7. People who don't smoke are either self-confident or cowards.

(10 contents, 10 correctness)

VI. Giving opinion

Imagine you have to write an article about drugs for an English school magazine.

1. Write about Ecstasy, alcohol and smoking **or** about any one of the three.
2. Suggest what could be done to prevent people from taking such drugs.

You might think of: being/getting addicted[1], reasons, friends, living conditions, spare time, dangers, costs, parents etc.

Write about 150 words altogether. Count your words. (25 p.)

[1] to be/get addicted to: abhängig sein/werden von

(15 contents, 10 correctness)

Lösung

I. Comprehension

1.

(1)	(2)	(3)	(4)	(5)	(6)
e	c	a	f	d	b

2. a) true   b) false
   c) false   d) false
   e) false   f) true
   g) true   h) false

II. Language

(1) schoolgirl, (2) hoped, (3) celebrate, (4) agreed, (5) trouble, (6) advises, (7) cared, (8) unconscious, (9) tablet, (10) sad, (11) courage

III. Grammar

1.

noun	verb	adjective
pleasure	to please	pleasurable
hope	to hope	hopeful/hopeless
depression	to depress	depressing/depressed/depressive
risk	to risk	risky

2. a) loudly b) fashionable
   c) happy d) terribly
   e) quickly

3. a) ..., less young people **will die**.
      (Hinweis: Hauptsatz = Simple Future Typ 1)
   b) ... if it **did not make** them ...
      (Hinweis: Nebensatz = Simple Past Typ 2)
   c) ..., fewer youngsters **would take** it.
      (Hinweis: Hauptsatz = would + Infinitiv Typ 2)

4. Antworten in folgender Reihenfolge
   Louise said that Ecstasy **made her** feel optimistic.
   Suddenly you **were** in a perfect world where everyone **loved** each other.
   She had never **felt** like that before.
   It **had been** absolutely fantastic.
   People **would not** stop taking "E".

5. Antworten in folgender Reihenfolge
   ... **have passed** since Leah's death ...
   (Hinweis: Signalwort = since, Simple Present Perfect)
   ... **died** last January.
   (Hinweis: Signalwort = last, Simple Past)
   ... often **went** to ...
   (Hinweis: Simple Past)
   ... wanted to **have** ...
   (Hinweis: Infinitive)
   ... **told** Scotland Yard yesterday ...
   (Hinweis: Signalwort = yesterday, Simple Past)
   ... he **had** never **taken** ...
   (Hinweis: Simple Past Perfect)
   Now he **is** ...
   (Hinweis: Simple Present)
   ... hope this **will keep** ...
   (Hinweis: Simple Future)

IV. **Using the language in different contexts**

Louise: "Why? I think you dance well."

Louise: "Well, why don't you take some dope? It will build you up."

Louise: "Of course not. I don't mean anything hard like cocaine. But try an Ecstasy tablet."

Louise: "Yes, I have. But she was unlucky because she didn't drink enough. You must drink a lot with the tablet."

Louise: "Well, I can't promise anything. There is always a tiny risk."

V. **Comment**

1. I don't think there are many youngsters taking drugs in our country.
   Quite the contrary. I am sure there are many youngsters taking drugs in our country. Young people have got worries and problems. You need only think of the high unemployment rate in our region. Many young people face problems they cannot solve. Sooner or later they feel an inclination (Neigung) to take drugs because they have heard of the wonderful effect. The option of escaping into a world without any problems is very attractive.

2. Ecstasy is dangerous for young people's lives.
   I agree with this statement. In my opinion, Ecstasy is one of the most dangerous drugs because it is said to be harmless. But this is a lie. Ecstasy is a new drug which damages nerve cells and changes the personality of a person. I feel sorry for all young people who think that Ecstasy is more acceptable than hard drugs like Heroin. They do not want to accept the long term effects.

3. Drugs are necessary if you want to have fun at a party.
   This statement is wrong. In my opinion, having fun at a party depends on the people coming to the party as well as the preparations for the party. The latest music, funny games, interesting conversation and a relaxed atmosphere can provide good entertainment. Drugs are unnecessary and dangerous.

4. Parents should teach their children how to handle alcohol.
   I disagree with this statement. Parents should keep an eye on their children and explain to them the dangers of alcohol. They are responsible for informing their kids about the risks. Drinking alcohol seems to be socially acceptable. It is legal and therefore youngsters and adults think it is harmless. However it is a drug and can lead to addiction like any other drug.

5. Schools and teenage magazines don't give enough information on drugs.
   This is not so. Teachers take every possible opportunity to offer information about the dangers of drugs, not only in biology lessons. Moreover school projects often deal with this problem too. In teenage magazines answers and advice are given by experts on the subject. However considering the growing consumption of drugs in schools, youth organizations, teenage magazies, and particularly the media in general should look for more convincing and effective methods of keeping young people informed about the dangers of drugs.

6. "E" kills fewer people than peanuts or sweets.
   I must contradict this statement. Peanuts and sweets are regularly consumed by many people. Although they may not be part of a healthy diet they can only lead to death

when they are consumed in large quantities over a long period of time. I don't think this happens very often. However there is no doubt about the deadly effects of Ecstasy. It damages nerve cells and ruins your health. Sooner or later the consumption of Ecstasy leads to death.

7. **People who don't smoke are either self-confident or cowards.**
I am a non-smoker but I do not consider myself to be a coward. Therefore I am convinced that non-smokers are self-confident people instead. Because so many people smoke it appears to be normal and socially acceptable to do so. Non-Smokers are often accused of not being trendy and "cool". Smokers often make fun of them. However this sort of behaviour doesn't usually make a non-smoker change his mind about smoking.

VI. Giving opinion

Useful words and phrases

to get addicted	süchtig werden
to be addictive	süchtig machen
to damage	zerstören/schädigen
to protect from	schützen vor
to prevent	verhindern
to face problems	Problemen gegenüber stehen
to feel an inclination	eine Neigung verspüren
to cause one's death	tödlich sein/den Tod verursachen
nerve cells	Nervenzellen
consumption of drugs	Drogenkonsum
confidence	Überzeugung/Zuversicht
effects	Auswirkungen

Ecstasy, alcohol, and nicotine are addictive and have got dangerous effects on one's health. In everyday life you can see people smoking and drinking alcohol. It seems to be normal. But can it be normal to destroy one's health and life?
Nowadays teenagers and even children are smoking. It starts as an adventure or a kind of hobby. They do not think of the risks and dangers. It's the same with alcohol. No party without beer or wine. Guests are always encouraged to drink, irrespective of age. One can only be in a good mood under the influence of alcohol. This is a widely spread opinion. However Ecstasy is the most serious threat to young people. It is said to be harmless and not as dangerous as hard drugs. That is definitely wrong. Ecstasy damages nerve cells and has serious long term effects.
Nicotine and alcohol destroy one's health, and can cause one's death after a long period of consumption. However the consumption of Ecstasy can cause death within a very short period of time.
What can be done to prevent people from taking such drugs?
I suggest passing stricter laws against the misuse of alcohol, nicotine and drugs. Cigarettes and alcoholic drinks should not be sold to youngsters under the age of 18. Discos, restaurants and all public institutions should be non-smoker zones. It is also necessary to create leisure time facilities for young people. An active young generation with sensible hobbies is better protected against such dangerous influences. That means the local authorities must provide money for youth clubs and sports centres.
Finally, all public institutions and media must do more to keep young people informed of the dangers of drugs, alcohol, and nicotine.

> **Realschulabschluss Englisch in Mecklenburg-Vorpommern**
> **Abschlussprüfung 1998**

Television

Are YOU a couch potato?
Do you like to sit down in front of the TV with your feet up, a bag of crisps on the table in front of you and a can of fizzy drink at your side? Well, you could be a candidate for the Couch Potato Club. This club really exists. It started in California and the club has members – thousands of them – all over the world. They believe that sitting in front of the TV for hours and hours is good for you. And to make life comfortable while they are watching, they eat and drink and eat and drink.
They watch TV for 16 to 18 hours a day, anything that's on the box. It's a strange and powerful addiction, similar to drug or alcohol addiction.
Obviously couch potatoes are very extreme, but even the average viewer in western countries watches TV for 30 hours a week.
TV has become a central part of many people's lives. With more and more TV channels and satellite stations people now have the opportunity to watch TV all day long.
By the age of 18, a child will have spent more time in front of the telly than at school. Just think of what they could achieve if they spent half the amount of TV time on homework, on reading good books, on outdoor activities or on sitting and talking with their families.
However, everybody knows that watching a lot of TV not only takes up your time but confronts you with both high and low quality television.
At prime time, for instance, which is the time between 7:00 and 11:00 p.m., when most youngsters are sitting in front of the television, crime, sex and violence dominate the programmes.
At other times people are hooked on[1] their daily soap operas that offer them a world different from their own, with pretty girls, handsome men and big cars. Unlike real life difficulties are always solved. It's the same with the problems in the commercials that interrupt the soaps so frequently. The problems shown there always have an easy solution that can be bought.
It's the non-commercial TV stations which try to put on more quality programmes, such as news and background information, educational series on arts, geography and science. They also show good, ambitious films which make people think.
Whether the quality of television is good or bad, the last word is always with the audience: if they don't like what they see, they can turn off the TV.

1 hooked on: süchtig sein nach

Aufgaben

I. Comprehension

1. Matching exercise. Combine the matching parts of the sentences: (6 p.)

   (1) Couch Potato Club members like watching TV,
   (2) The club has members
   (3) Watching TV for 16–18 hours a day
   (4) A teenager of 18 has spent more hours watching TV
   (5) Low quality TV
   (6) Soap operas don't show

   a) the difficulties of real life.
   b) than working for school.
   c) in every part of the world.
   d) is a strange and powerful addiction.
   e) eating crisps and drinking.
   f) dominates at prime time.

   Put the correct letters below the numbers.

(1)	(2)	(3)	(4)	(5)	(6)

2. Read the text carefully. Find out which statements are true and which are false. Mark with a cross. (9 p.)

   true | false

   a) California is the birthplace of the Couch Potato Club.
   b) While they are watching TV they forget to eat and drink.
   c) Members of the Couch Potato Club are addicted to drugs.
   d) Because of today's high number of TV channels and satellite stations people can watch TV as long as they want to.
   e) Children under 18 spend more time in front of the telly at school than at home.
   f) At prime time the programme is not very educational.
   g) Commercials tell people that they can buy a solution of their problems.
   h) The commercial TV stations broadcast more news and background information than the non-commercial ones.
   i) The viewers can decide if they watch good or bad programmes.

II. Language

From the words below choose the suitable ones and fill in the gaps. (11 p.)

them – upset – proud of – listening – something – during – under – their – while – independent – waste – usually – tired of – cartoons – carefully – to know – are – agree – satellite – screen

Western societies are (1) _____ their freedom of speech and their (2) _____ media. But there is also a negative side.
For example, children (3) _____ 15 are among the keenest TV viewers. Both in the United Kingdom and the United States, they sit in front of the (4) _____ for about 5 hours a day.
They are (5) _____ not much interested in documentaries, feature films or discussion programmes. They prefer watching commercials, (6) _____ and action films.
Several groups of people complain that the media (7) _____ full of sex and violence.
Others argue that people have a right (8) _____ what is going on around (9) _____.
Most people, however, (10) _____ that not everything can be shown on TV, especially (11) _____ the main viewing times for children.

III. Grammar

1. Fill in the correct words. (8 p.)

noun	verb	adjective
	to dominate	
		various
	to talk	
comparison		

2. Adjective or adverb? (6 p.)
   Put in the correct forms.
   Here are some slogans you can hear in the commercials.
   a) Buy FRUITIES for a _____ (happy) family.
   b) These clothes are _____ (extreme) comfortable – so get our STRETCHO.
   c) Take WRINKLESS and your skin looks _____ (beautiful).
   d) NIKESHOES _____ (sure) win the competition.
   e) Here are MINTS for a _____ (fresh) taste.
   f) Live more _____ (active) – join the TEEVEE sports club.

3. If clauses (3 p.)
   Please fill in the correct forms.
   If there weren't so many TV channels and satellite stations, people _____ (watch) less TV.
   The quality of television would be better if the commercials _____ (not interrupt) the programmes so frequently.
   You can earn a lot of money through advertising if you _____ (be) a successful sportsman.

4. Passive (6 p.)
   Please put the verbs in brackets into the passive voice.
   Here is some information that was released by a Disney PR manager.
   In the thirties the Walt Disney Film Company _____ (build up).
   From the start, Disney's films were very successful and since then they _____ (show) so often that nowadays Mickey Mouse _____ (know) all over the world.
   Today not only Disney videos but all kinds of Mickey Mouse products _____ (buy) by millions of fans.
   Mickey Mouse is more popular than ever, he _____ really _____ (love) by everybody.
   Last year Mickey Mouse _____ (choose) "Mascot of the Year."

5. Tenses (8 p.)
   Please put the verbs in brackets into the correct tense.
   Nowadays most people _____ (have) a television set in their homes.
   In some houses you _____ (find) two or three, or even more!
   Fifty years ago things _____ (be) different.
   The number of television viewers _____ (grow) greatly since 1960.
   Since that time there _____ also _____ (be) many developments in television technology.
   In the past everything _____ (appear) in black and white.
   Today we _____ (expect) to see our programmes in colour and sometimes with stereo sound.
   In the future these developments _____ (continue).

IV. Using the language in different contexts (18 p.)

Defective dialogue

Imagine a TV reporter is doing an interview in the street asking you some questions. Please answer in complete sentences.

Reporter: How much TV do you watch a day?
You: _____

Reporter: What are your favourite programmes and why do you like them?
You: _____

Reporter: What do you think of documentaries and educational programmes?
You: _____

Reporter: Are there any programmes that are bad for children? Can you give any examples?
You: _____

Reporter: Do you think parents should regulate the amount of TV they let their children watch? Give reasons.
You: _____

Reporter: How do you like commercials? Why?
You: _____

V. Comment

Comment on *two* of the following statements. Write about 80 words altogether. Count your words. (20 p.)

1. Watching violence on the screen leads to violence in real life.
2. TV kills conversation.
3. Watching TV is a waste of time.
4. People are better informed because of TV.
5. Watching TV is like taking drugs.
6. TV viewers are fat – sportsmen are fit.

VI. Giving opinion (25 p.)

An English teenage magazine has started a discussion on the media. The editorial team asks its readers:

> WHAT INFLUENCE
> DO THE MEDIA HAVE
> ON OUR LIVES?

Write to the magazine and discuss the advantages <u>and</u> disadvantages of TV and/or other media.

You might think of entertainment, education, advertisements, sex and violence, paparazzi, information, laziness, babysitter ...

Write about 150 words altogether. Count your words.

Lösung

I. Comprehension

1.

(1)	(2)	(3)	(4)	(5)	(6)
e	c	d	b	f	a

2. a) true b) false
   c) false d) true
   e) false f) true
   g) true h) false
   i) true

II. Language

Antworten in folgender Reihenfolge:

(1) proud of, (2) independent, (3) under, (4) screen, (5) usually, (6) cartoons, (7) are, (8) to know, (9) them, (10) agree, (11) during

III. Grammar

1.

noun	verb	adjective
dominance	to dominate	**dominant**
variety	**to vary**	various
talk	to talk	**talkative**
comparison	**to compare**	**comparable**

2. a) happy b) extremely
   c) beautiful d) surely
   e) fresh f) actively

3. ... people **would watch** less TV.
   (Hinweis: NS = Simple Past /, HS = Would + Infinitive)

   ... if the commercials **didn't interrupt** ...
   (Hinweis: HS = Would + Infinitive /, NS = Simple Past)

   ... if you **are** a successful ...
   (Hinweis: HS = Future /, NS = Simple Present)

4. Antworten in folgender Reihenfolge:

... the Walt Disney Film Company **was built up**.
(Hinweis: Signalwort = in the thirties, Simple Past)

... and since then they **have been shown** so ...
(Hinweis: Signalwort = since, Simple Present Perfect)

... that nowadays Mickey Mouse **is known** all ...
(Hinweis: Signalwort = nowadays, Simple Present)

... products **are bought** by ...
(Hinweis: Signalwort = today, Simple Present)

... he **is** really **loved** by ...
(Hinweis: Allgemeingültige Aussage, Simple Present)

... Mickes Mouse **was chosen** ...
(Hinweis: Signalwort = last year, Simple Past)

5. Antworten in folgender Reihenfolge:

... most people **have** a television set ...
(Hinweis: Signalwort = nowadays, Simple Present)

... you **find** two ...
(Hinweis: Allgemeingültige Aussage, Simple Present)

... things **were** different.
(Hinweis: Signalwort = ago, Simple Past)

... viewers **has grown** greatly ...
(Hinweis: Signalwort = since, Simple Present Perfect)

... there **have** also **been** many ...
(Hinweis: Signalwort = since, Simple Present Perfect)

... everything **appeared** in ...
(Hinweis: Signalwort = in the past, Simple Past)

... we **expect** to see ...
(Hinweis: Signalwort = today, Simple Present)

... these developments **will continue.**
(Hinweis: Signalwort = in the future, Simple Future)

IV. Using the language in different contexts

You: "I usually watch TV between two and three hours a day."
You: "My favourite programmes are documentaries and game shows because they are exciting and informative."
You: "I think they are interesting and useful."
You: "Many cartoons and science fiction films, for example, are full of violent scenes and that's why they are bad for children."
You: "Yes, I think so. Children can be easily influenced. That's why they should spend their spare time with more useful things instead of watching too much TV."
You: "Sometimes I like commercials because they can be really funny. But I hate them when they interrupt exciting programmes."

V. Comment

1. Watching violence on the screen leads to violence in real life.
   Unfortunately I must agree with this statement. There are a lot of daily incidents which show that violence on the screen can cause aggression in real life. Especially children and teenagers can be easily influenced. They often take movie action heroes as an example and think they must solve the problems they have with each other violently and aggressively.

2. TV kills conversation.
   I must contradict this statement because I do not think it is TV that kills a conversation but the people watching it. It always depends on the individual whether he/she is interested in a good talk or not. Switching the TV set off is necessary in order to start a conversation.

3. Watching TV is a waste of time.
   I can only partly agree with this statement. In my opinion, watching TV is only a waste of time if you always watch programmes of a very low standard. Actually, there are a lot of broadcasts which inform and entertain viewers at a high standard and broaden people's knowledge.

4. People are better informed because of TV.
   To my mind, TV is only one of the media informing people well and quickly. But I suppose TV is in favour with the people because audiovisual impressions are more comfortably received. That's why viewers are informed as well as newspaper readers or radio listeners.

5. Watching TV is like taking drugs.
   I would say watching TV can be addictive. Therefore there is a connection between taking drugs and watching TV. But drug addiction is more dangerous and more destructive for people because it can even cause death. Fortunately, I have not heard yet that a TV addict died.

6. TV viewers are fat – sportsmen are fit.
   I can only partly agree with this statement. There is no doubt that sportsmen are fit because they go in for sports regularly. As sportsmen are often interested in sports competitions taking place all the time all over the world they are also very often TV viewers, but not fat. Therefore I think such a generalization is stupid.

VI. Giving opinion

Useful words and phrases

information	Information/en
news	Nachrichten
to inform/to be informed	informieren/informiert werden
to receive	erhalten
to entertain	unterhalten
entertainment	Unterhaltung
influence	Einfluss
to influence/to be influenced	beeinflussen/beeinflusst werden
to broadcast	ausstrahlen/senden
broadcast	Sendung
violent	gewalttätig

aggressive   aggressiv
high /low standard   hohes /niedriges Niveau
impressions   Eindrücke

Life without the media is unthinkable today. Therefore the media have a stronger influence on our lives than we want to admit.

The media make our existence more interesting, more exciting, more informative and more varied.

However, a large variety of media people often prefer watching TV for information and entertainment. I suppose audiovisual impressions are more comfortably received. But like all things have two sides TV also has both advantages and disadvantages.

Watching TV can be very useful. There are a lot of programmes with a high standard of education to enlarge viewers' knowledge, for example. With the help of TV you can be in any place in the world at any time. You can get information about everything concerning our lives. However, there are also disadvantages. In my opinion, TV is a danger to human relations. More and more you can see people (and especially children) sitting in front of the TV set in their spare time instead of spending time with their family or friends. Furthermore, too many violent programmes are broadcasted at times when youngsters usually watch TV. Cartoons or science fiction films are sometimes full of violent scenes. Children are easily influenced and think there is no difference between TV and real life and that brutality is normal.

In conclusion, I think the media influence our lives but it depends on the individual whether this influence is positive or negative.

Fans

"I couldn't survive without music," says fifteen-year-old Steve. In the morning, Steve wakes up to his favourite radio station. He listens to rock on the radio while he eats breakfast. He puts on his Walkman before he leaves the house and listens to cassettes on the bus to school. "Last week I put my headphones on in the maths class," admits Steve. "The
5 teacher was really angry. She took my headphones away and I couldn't use them for a week. It was terrible." At home Steve does his homework to music. Loud music. "My mother always shouts 'turn it down!'" says Steve. "She can't understand how I can work with music on, but music helps me to concentrate."

For teenagers like Steve, music is a very important part of life. Music is social. It brings
10 people together at discos, parties and concerts. That's why everyone likes it so much. It gives pleasure to teenagers and voices their thoughts, hopes, fears and feelings.
Fast loud music is full of energy. It helps people to forget their problems and have fun. Music talks about love, freedom and imagination. There are always new songs and new styles.

15 But there can be a negative side to rock music as well, because it's not only a harmless way to relax and have fun. Dr. A. Handforth has some serious concerns.

"Music on a Walkman is often too loud," she says. "It can damage your hearing. Also, other people on buses and trains may not want to listen to your cassette of 'Aerosmith'. Personal stereos stop you noticing the world outside. And of course, some sorts of music
20 create aggression and violence." – Steve agrees. He adds, "I'm also worried that friends of mine take Ecstasy at rave parties although they know how dangerous it is."

Many parents are concerned about discos starting very late in the evening and not ending until early in the morning. Young girls make their way home in the dark. Statistics show that this is risky and provokes crime. That's why 70 per cent of US cities and towns have
25 introduced curfew[1] laws, forbidding teenagers to be on the streets after 10 p.m. at night.

Steve's mother thinks that music brings different problems. "Steve is a sensible boy," she says. "I don't think he would ever take drugs or turn violent at night after the disco. But I do worry about his hearing with all that loud music. It drives me crazy! And he shouldn't spend all his pocket money on it."

30 There's the question of money. Most teenage fans don't just enjoy rock and pop – they spend a lot of money on CDs, videos, posters, magazines or concert tickets. Being a music fan is more than just listening to music.

[1] Ausgangssperre

Aufgaben

I. Comprehension

1. Matching exercise. Combine the matching parts of the sentences. (6 p.)

   (1) Steve thinks he
   (2) He listens to music
   (3) Steve complains that
   (4) Dr. Handforth says that
   (5) Teenagers spend a lot of money
   (6) Going home in the dark

   a) some music can lead to aggressive and violent behaviour.
   b) can't live without music.
   c) on everything that has to do with music.
   d) is risky for girls.
   e) he had to give his headphones to his maths teacher.
   f) even on his way to school.

(1)	(2)	(3)	(4)	(5)	(6)

2. Read the text carefully. Find out which statements are true and which are false. Mark with a cross. (8 p.)

true	false	
		1. Steve always listens to the radio when he has breakfast.
		2. His maths teacher has not given him his headphones back yet.
		3. Music helps young people when they have problems.
		4. Dr. A. Handforth says loud music on the headphones causes hearing problems.
		5. Loud music may disturb people on public transport.
		6. Everywhere in the USA teenagers are forbidden to be on the streets after a certain time at night.
		7. Steve's mother doesn't like his loud music.
		8. She thinks that Steve spends his pocket money on drugs.

II. Language

From the words below choose the suitable ones and fill in the gaps. (11 p.)

age – agree – are – between – earning – happiest – how – in – many – environment – problems – to listen – to pay – worry – youngsters

Youth (1) _____ have often been discussed in recent years. Teenagers (2) _____ about their grades at school, the effects of drug use, being robbed or attacked, the pollution of the (3) _____ etc. Nowadays, finding a job and (4) _____ money are of high interest for (5) _____. There are (6) _____ things teenagers need money for. The pocket money they get from their parents is often not enough (7) _____ for everything. Most British teenagers get (8) _____ £4 and £5 a week. At the (9) _____ of 13 some already have part-time jobs. Music is one of the most important things (10) _____ many teenagers' lives. Other popular activities (11) _____ sport, computer games, going to the cinema, watching TV and reading.

Getting my ears pierced was cool. Getting my nose pierced was cool. Getting my tongue pierced was cool. Getting my eyes pierced was a bad idea.

Copyright 1996 Randy Glasbergen. www.glasbergen.com

III. Grammar

1. Fill in the correct words. (8 p.)

noun	verb	adjective
	to free	
care		
		imaginable
success		

2. Adjective – Comparison. Put in the correct forms. (8 p.)

   15-year-old Joe has got a _____ (good) part-time job. He's doing a paper round in the morning before school. This is _____ (easy) than babysitting and he gets about as _____ (much) money as his friend who helps out in a shop. From the money Joe buys "Smash Hits", the _____ (popular) music magazine you can find in Britain.

   For him "Chat" is not so _____ (attractive) as "Smash hits". He also enjoys dancing in the _____ (hot) discos in town and loves inviting the _____ (beautiful) girls you've ever seen for a meal. There is nothing _____ (bad) than boredom in a teenager's life.

3. If clauses. Please fill in the correct forms. (3 p.)

   a) If Steve _____ to that fast loud music all day, he will get problems with his hearing. (listen)

   b) If teenagers _____ music so much, they wouldn't spend a lot of money on CDs. (not enjoy)

   c) Many parents in Germany _____ if the towns and cities introduced stricter laws for teenagers. (agree)

4. Questions. At a disco. The music is very loud. Here and there you can hear people ask for more information. **Complete their questions.** (5 p.)

   a) "Oh, that boy is looking at us!"
      "Who _____?"

   b) "Steve listens to music a lot."
      "How often _____?"

   c) "Last night she left the disco very late."
      "At what time _____?"

   d) "Gary will have his own flat soon."
      "When _____?"

   e) "Sue hasn't met him for a long time."
      "Why _____?"

5. Tenses. Please put the verbs in brackets into the correct tense. (8 p.)

   Glastonbury is a three-day festival that _____ (take) place every year at the end of June. Usually, rock and pop _____ (be) the main attractions. But last year you _____ (can) also find a cinema tent and a circus. About 2,000 people _____ (come) to the first Glastonbury Festival in 1970 and many of them _____ (get) in without paying – they just climbed over the fences. Since then local people _____ (try) to stop the festival because of the noise and security problems.

Every year in June also many parents are worried: Glastonbury _____ (not have) enough washing or toilet facilities, the music is extremely loud and all those crazy youngsters sleep together in huge tents. Their children, however, hope that the festival _____ (bring) them pleasure again the next year.

IV. Using the language in different contexts

Defective dialogue: Interview. (18 p.)

A British reporter has come to your school. You are with your friends and he starts asking you questions.

Reporter: What is a real friend for you?
You: _____

Reporter: What are your favourite spare-time activities?
You: _____

Reporter: How much pocket money do you get and what do you spend it on?
You: _____

Reporter: Where can young people spend their spare time here in this area?
You: _____

Reporter: What do you think of drugs and alcohol at parties?
You: _____

Reporter: What do your parents worry about when you are out late at night?
You: _____

V. Comment

Comment on **two** of the following statements. Write about 80 words altogether.

(20 p.)

- There is a strong connection between some kinds of music and drug taking.
- Music should be played loudly.
- Rock bands can create feelings of aggression and violence.
- Music is an escape from the problems and boredom of everyday life.
- Parents shouldn't allow teenagers under 18 to stay out longer than midnight.
- Curfews protect teenagers. Let's introduce them in Germany.
- Modern music is a harmless way to relax and have fun.

VI. Giving opinion

There is a survey in a British youth magazine about the differences between British youngsters and teenagers from other countries. The magazine wants to find out:

> ARE TEENAGERS' PROBLEMS AND PLEASURES INTERNATIONAL?

Write a letter to contribute to their survey.
Introduce yourself and say where you come from. Explain what you like best about your life and what worries you most. Try to give reasons. Write about 150 words altogether.
(You might think of: music, love, friendship, parents, school, spare time, pocket money, fashion, media, jobs, violence, environment, ...)

(25 p.)

Lösung

I. Comprehension

1.

(1)	(2)	(3)	(4)	(5)	(6)
b	f	e	a	c	d

2. a) true   b) false
   c) true   d) true
   e) true   f) false
   g) true   h) false

II. Language

(1) problems, (2) worry, (3) environment, (4) earning, (5) youngsters, (6) many, (7) to pay, (8) between, (9) age, (10) in, (11) are

III. Grammar

1.

noun	verb	adjective
freedom	**to free**	**free**
care	**to care**	careful/careless
imagination	**to imagine**	imaginable
success	**to succeed**	**successful**

2. a) good   b) easier
   c) much   d) most popular
   e) attractive   f) hottest/hot
   g) most beautiful   h) worse

3. a) If Steve **listens** to that…
     (Hinweis: Nebensatz = Simple Present Typ 1)

   b) If teenagers **did not enjoy** music so…
     (Hinweis: Nebensatz = Simple Past Typ 2)

   c) Many parents in Germany **would agree** if the…
     (Hinweis: Hauptsatz = would + Infinitiv Typ 2)

4. Fragen in folgender Reihenfolge

   a) Who **is looking at us/you? /is he looking at?**

   b) How often **does Steve/he listen to music?**

   c) At what time **did she leave the disco?**

d) When **will Gary/he have his own flat/it?**
e) Why **hasn't Sue/she met him for a long time?**

5. Antworten in folgender Reihenfolge

...that **takes** place every year...
(Hinweis: Signalwort = every year, Simple Present)

...rock and pop **are** the main...
(Hinweis: Signalwort = usually, Simple Present)

...last year you **could** also find...
(Hinweis: Signalwort = last year, Simple Past)

...people **came** to the...
(Hinweis: Signalwort = in1970, Simple Past)

...them **got** in without...
(Hinweis: Signalwort = in1970, Simple Past)

...local people **have tried** to stop...
(Hinweis: Signalwort = since then, Simple Present Perfect)

...**does not have** enough...
(Hinweis: Signalwort = every year, Simple Present)

...the festival **will bring** them...
(Hinweis: Signalwort = hope, Simple Future)

IV. Using the language in different contexts

You: "A real friend for me is a person I can trust and rely on."
You: "My favourite spare time activities are meeting friends and playing sports."
You: "I get DM 10 a week and I spend it on fees for the fitness club and sometimes on sweets."
You: "Young people can spend their spare time in several youth clubs or sports centres."
You: "In my opinion, drugs and alchohol are not necessary at parties."
You: They worry about where I am and how I am getting home.

V. Comment

1. There is a strong connection between some kinds of music and drug taking.
I am afraid I have to agree. In fact, the development of the rave music scene is very closely connected with the consumption of drugs, especially Ecstasy. This drug circulates at marathon rave dance parties because taking it avoids getting tired and produces a feeling of extreme happiness.

2. **Music should be played loudly.**
   Although I know that many people, including some of my friends, think that music must be played loudly, I'm of a different opinion because of reasons of health. It is a sad fact that the hearing of many, not only young people, has got worse during the last few years because of music played loudly, for instance in discos.

3. **Rock bands can create feelings of aggression and violence.**
   In my opinion, rock bands want to pass on information to the audience with their music and they want to create feelings. It depends on the intention of the band what message is passed on and what feelings are created. Therefore, I think there are bands creating feelings like aggression and violence as well as bands creating emotions of joy and happiness.

4. **Music is an escape from the problems and boredom of everyday life.**
   I can only partly agree with this statement. I think life without music is boring. Music can help you to relax and to forget problems or conflicts for a while but it is not possible for a person who is realistic to permanently escape problems in this way.

5. **Parents shouldn't allow teenagers under 18 to stay out longer than midnight.**
   I want to emphasize that parents should forbid teenagers under 18 to stay out longer than midnight. It is a sad fact that more and more teenagers fall victim to crime at night. It is risky and dangerous walking home in the dark, for instance after discos. Parents are responsible for protecting their children from danger and that is why they have to get them to agree to returning home before midnight.

6. **Curfews protect teenagers. Let's introduce them in Germany.**
   To my mind, such laws would not be necessary if parents did not allow their children under 18 to stay out longer than midnight. Therefore, I think it is useful to strenghten parents' confidence to bring their children up to accept this.

7. **Modern music is a harmless way to relax and have fun.**
   This saying seems to be true. For me, music is not only a harmless, but also a simple and pleasant way to relax and to have fun. After an exhausting day music helps me to relax and to get into a good mood. Furthermore, I think that music brings people together everywhere and at any time.

VI. Giving opinion

Useful words and phrases

to owe s.o. s.th.	–	jmdm. etw. verdanken
to be strict	–	streng sein
to trust s.o.	–	jmdm. trauen
to rely on s.o.	–	sich auf jmdn. verlassen
to apply for a job	–	sich bewerben
to be suitable	–	geeignet sein
to fall victim to…	–	Opfer werden von…
to accompany s.o.	–	jmdn. begleiten

Dear magazine, 29th July, 1999

It was very interesting for me to read about your survey. Therefore, I want to contribute my thoughts to your study. But first let me introduce myself. My name is Katharina Will and I am 16 years old. I live in Schwerin, and at the moment I'm preparing for my final examinations. Well, what I like best about my life is having my parents and my friends. I owe a very loving upbringing to my mother and my father. Although they are sometimes strict, they show a lot of patience with me and my faults. They always stand by me.

Every day I meet a lot of people, but only a few I call friends. I have chosen them very carefully. I can trust them and rely on them. We share a lot of interests and enjoy life. But there are also things which really worry me.

I think it is very difficult to find out which job might be the right one for me. I have applied for jobs several times but I have not found an apprenticeship yet. Next week I will have an interview at a lawyer's office, and I hope I will be suitable for this job.

Another thing I worry about is the growing pollution and destruction of our environment. A lot of damage has already been done to human health and nature. I am often angry with people because of their carelessness.

Furthermore, I am afraid of falling victim to crime. The risk of attack has become very high in recent years. It is risky going home in the dark and that's why my friends and I try to arrange for someone to accompany us home from the discos.

In conclusion, I would like to say that my youth is a very happy time but it is far from being a time without conflicts, worries and sorrows.

Yours faithfully,

Katharina Will

Realschulabschluss Englisch in Mecklenburg-Vorpommern
Abschlussprüfung 2000: Listening Comprehension

In the following listening comprehension test you will hear about three different aspects of teenage life.

Aufgabe 1: Money, Money

For many young people money is very important in their lives. This was found out in a survey of 10,000 British children, who were between 6 and 16 years old.
We've done some interviews to find out more about this and talked to Martin. He said, "Music is the most important thing in my life. If I worry about anything, it's about the money I need to buy CDs and music magazines. You should know that I spend more than £50 every month on music. My parents give me £5 every week, which is not really enough.
Most of my friends have computer games, stereos and TVs in their rooms. Some of them even have refrigerators, and they get more pocket money than I do. That's why I also have a job: in the morning I do paper rounds and take newspapers to different houses or flats. Sometimes at the weekends and in the evenings I even do babysitting to make some money and my parents pay me for household jobs such as cutting the grass and washing the car.
You see a music fan's life is quite hard ..."

Aufgabe 2: An Active Life

Everybody loves to have free time for themselves. Today we want to ask a teenager how he spends his spare time. Dave is 16. He told us that he liked an active life.
"You know, working for my exams is the most important thing for me at the moment, but I still have enough time for my hobbies and sports. My homework takes about half an hour to an hour every day. I hate sitting down all day at school, and so when I've finished my homework, I usually go jogging in the park.
It's a good way of getting school out of my head. On Wednesday evenings, I play the guitar in a band. It's really relaxing and a lot of fun. We enjoy playing our own songs even more than listening to modern music on the radio. At the weekends I like being active, too. I go swimming every Saturday morning and on Sunday afternoons I usually play football with my friends. On Sunday mornings I always take my dog for a long walk and if the weather is good, my friends and I ride our bikes up to Black Rock and go climbing there. That's really exciting and we love it. Some people might say that I do too much sport at weekends, but I couldn't just stay in and watch TV. Most programmes are boring and not very attractive for me anyway. I want to live my life."

Aufgabe 3: No School? That's Cool!

Almost two million kids in the United States don't go to school anymore. Instead, their parents teach them at home. Home schooling is legal in the United States – and a big trend. What is home schooling like?
No more homework or tests. No more mean teachers. No more bus rides on cold, wet mornings. No more playground bullies or bad school lunches. – Doesn't that sound great? Not every child, however, is happy with mum as their private maths teacher. You sit at the same kitchen table for hours each day. Your mother tells you what, when and how to study. If you have brothers and sisters you are with them seven days a week. This could surely get on your nerves.

There are four times as many home-schooled boys and girls now than were ten years ago. In 1990 there were only 300,000 kids who were taught by their parents. But more and more parents are unhappy with American public schools: with violence on the classroom and the growing number of drugs. The most important reason parents in Florida gave for home schooling was safety.

In the past, there were US laws against home schooling. But parents fought to have them changed. Now all US states allow parents to teach their children at home.

Aufgabe 1: Money, Money (6 p)

Today's special radio programme for young people in the London area deals with the problem of pocket money. Listen to the report and tick ☑ the correct information. There is only one answer per item.

1. A survey of ten thousand children was made in
   - ☐ Germany.
   - ☐ Britain.
   - ☐ the USA.

2. Martin needs money, because he wants to buy
   - ☐ computer games.
   - ☐ a CD-player.
   - ☐ music magazines.

3. From his parents Martin gets
   - ☐ £5 a week.
   - ☐ £50 a month.
   - ☐ £50 a week.

4. Martin's friends have got
   - ☐ more pocket money.
   - ☐ less pocket money.
   - ☐ the same.

5. Martin does babysitting
   - ☐ every day.
   - ☐ in the mornings.
   - ☐ now and then at the weekends.

6. Martin's parents pay him for
   - ☐ washing the car.
   - ☐ babysitting.
   - ☐ doing paper rounds.

Aufgabe 2: An Active Life

The same special radio programme discussed the problem of young people and their spare time. Listen to the report and tick whether the following information is true or false. ☑ (7 p)

	true	false
1. Dave has not enough time for sports.	☐	☐
2. Every day he needs one hour for his homework	☐	☐
3. Before doing his homework, Dave usually goes jogging.	☐	☐
4. On Wednesdays he plays in a band.	☐	☐
5. Dave has a dog.	☐	☐
6. At the weekends he wants to relax at home.	☐	☐
7. Dave finds most TV programmes boring.	☐	☐

Aufgabe 3: No school? – That's cool!

Not long ago this programme gave some information about schools in the USA. There have been some errors during broadcasting. Correct them. (7 p)

1. Almost two million kids in the United States don't go to school anymore.

2. Instead, their parents meet them at home. Home schooling is legal in the

3. United States – and a big trend.

4. What is home schooling like?

5. No more homework or tests. No more mean teachers. No more bus drivers

6. on cold, wet mornings. No more playground bullies or bad school lunches.

7. – Doesn't that sound great? Not every child, however, is happy with mum

8. as their private maths teacher. You sit at the same kitchen table for hours

9. every day. Your mother tells you what, when and how to study.

10. If you have brothers or sisters you are with them seven days a week.

11. This could surely get on your nerves.

12. There are four times as many home-schooled boys and girls now than

13. there were twenty years ago. In 1990 there were only 30,000 kids who

14. were taught by their parents. But more and more parents are unhappy with

15. American public schools: with violence in the classroom and the growing

16. number of deaths. The most important reason parents in Florida gave for

17. home schooling was safety. In the past, there were US laws against home

18. schooling. But parents forgot to have them changed. Now all US states

19. allow parents to teach their children at home.

Lösung

Aufgabe 1

1. Britain
2. music magazines
3. £5 a week
4. more pocket money
5. now and then at the weekends
6. washing the car

Aufgabe 2

1 f, 2 f, 3 f, 4 t, 5 t, 6 f, 7 t

Aufgabe 3

	falsch	richtig
Zeile 2	meet	teach
Zeile 5	drivers	rides
Zeile 9	every	each
Zeile 13	twenty	ten
Zeile 13	30,000	300,000
Zeile 16	deaths	drugs
Zeile 18	forgot	fought

> Realschulabschluss Englisch in Mecklenburg-Vorpommern
> Abschlussprüfung 2000: Reading Comprehension

The Truth About Kids Today

What is it like to be a young person today? Earlier this year, *The Guardian* decided to find out. Over 500 children between the ages of 11 and 15 living throughout Britain were asked about their likes, dislikes, their hopes and thoughts.

The survey shows that the one thing young people are most worried about is their chance of getting a job when they leave school (72 per cent). Suzanne Lucas, 11, who lives with her unemployed mother and sister in Edinburgh, would not like to end up like her mother. "She's split up with my Dad and she's got no job and she's got two children to look after," Suzanne explained to *The Guardian*. "I really want to get a good education and finish school. Today, without good qualifications, they won't even accept you as a trainee."
In Britain, youngsters spend most of the day at school, from 9 a.m. to 4 p.m. Evenings are usually not free, as there is homework to do; an average of about one and a half hours a night for this age group. According to the survey, the rest of the time is divided between playing with friends or family, listening to music and, above all, watching TV or videos. In fact, young people watch TV 11 hours 45 minutes a week on average. That is six times longer than they spend reading, writes *The Guardian*.
According to the survey, youngsters receive about £5.25 pocket money a week. That's why shopping is another popular activity among young people. They spend their money on clothes, CDs, magazines, tickets for concerts or the cinema and computer equipment. Nearly three hours a week they spend playing computer games. "I think you have to learn about computers if you are going to get a job these days," explained 15-year-old Mark who would like to work for a computer firm near his home town, Manchester.
Bullying is a very serious problem in British schools. The survey found that more than half the children were bullied, usually because of their appearance. "If you don't look good you can get into trouble at school. There's a fat kid in our class and he is called 'Fatty'. If you wear sports clothes without a name on them like Adidas, you get bullied," Max Jackson, 15, explained.
Drugs are also a problem in secondary schools. One in three 11- to 15-year-olds said someone had offered them drugs and one in ten had taken them. Most said they felt they knew enough about the danger of drug use.
"I've been offered hash", Roxanne admitted, "but I haven't taken it. A girl I know died four months ago. It was probably heroin. Leah Betts is the one that took Ecstasy – people take it at raves. I think it's very good that such drugs are not legal. They're worse than alcohol and it worries me that the stuff is even sold in our school playground."

Aufgaben

I. Comprehension

1. Matching exercise. Combine the matching parts of the sentences: (6 p.)

   (1) More than 500 British children took part in
   (2) An 11-year-old girl doesn't want
   (3) Watching TV is
   (4) Shopping and playing computer games are
   (5) A lot of the children were bullied
   (6) A young girl probably died

   a) the most popular evening activity.
   b) because of their looks.
   c) other leisure activities among young British.
   d) because of heroin.
   e) a survey.
   f) a life like her mother's.

(1)	(2)	(3)	(4)	(5)	(6)

2. Read the text carefully. Find out which statements are true and which are false. Mark with a cross. (8 p.)

true	false	
		a) 500 children asked *The Guardian* questions.
		b) Only 72 per cent of the children see a chance of getting a job.
		c) All British children spend less than one and a half hours on homework every night.
		d) British youngsters like watching TV or videos better than reading.
		e) 15-year-old Mark thinks computer knowledge is necessary to get a job nowadays.
		f) Max Jackson is bullied because he is fat.
		g) Every third pupil between the ages of 11 and 15 has already taken illegal drugs
		h) Teenagers in Britain can't buy illegal drugs.

II. Language

From the words below choose the suitable ones and fill in the gaps. (11 p.)

homeless – of having – prison – their – responsible – culture – different – situation – to – afraid – money – dream – selling – away – for

For many teenagers in the USA, Hollywood seems like an escape from (1) _____ difficult home lives. They don't know where to look (2) _____ help and the only way out of the situation is to run (3) _____ from it.

They go to Hollywood with the (4) _____ of becoming movie stars and (5) _____ a glamorous lifestyle.

However, Hollywood's reality is that thieves steal the youngsters' (6) _____, and many of them soon become involved in buying and (7) _____ drugs.

They do all this in order (8) _____ survive.

Some teenagers even become gang members and end up in (9) _____ because they are violent and commit crimes.

Others lead a miserable life on the streets and are always (10) _____ of violence.

So all the dreams the teenagers have when they arrive in Hollywood and the reality they find there are very (11) _____ from each other.

III. Grammar

1. Fill in the correct words. (8 p.)

noun	verb	adjective
		active
	to hope	
	to legalize	
respect		

2. Adjective – Comparison: Put in the correct forms (8 p.)

British teachers are worried about their pupils' fitness. Teenagers aren't as _____ (fit) as they were twenty years ago.

Everybody knows that today children are taken everywhere by car, and going by bus is _____ (popular) than walking.

That's why teenagers nowadays don't have regular exercise which is the _____ (important) thing for keeping fit and healthy.

For many kids, computer games are _____ (exciting) than running around in the playground. But they become the _____ (lazy) people in front of their computers.

In addition to that, a lot of children spend _____ (much) time on homework than on sport.

70 % of all teenagers do _____ (little) than two hours of sport a week.

You see, school sport doesn't play a _____ (serious) role in a pupil's life.

3. If clauses. Please fill in the correct forms. (3 p.)

   a) If teenagers work hard at school, they _____ (have) a good chance of getting a job.

   b) Many kids could work more actively at school if they _____ (watch) less TV.

   c) Most young people _____ (not worry) if there were better opportunity for vocational training.

4. Questions (5 p.)
In Roxanne's youth club a street-worker talks to the girl about her experiences with drugs. He asks her questions to get more information.

   a) Only yesterday somebody offered me some hash in our school playground.
   Who _____ ?

   b) My friend, Steve, even took hash in our youth club.
   When _____ ?

   c) But I don't take it.
   Why _____ ?

   d) I have already tried drugs.
   Which drugs _____ ?

   e) I think I will spend my pocket money more sensibly.
   How _____ ?

5. Tenses. Please put the verbs in brackets into the correct tense. (8 p.)

This year, 16-year-old Kristy Lawson _____ (attend) Cranford High School.
She _____ (finish) school next term. The girl _____ already _____ (apply) for a job. Last week she _____ (have) an interview. But the firm _____ (not send) her their decision yet.

Although Kristy _____ (work) hard for school every day, she spends hours listening to music. She has a fantastic collection of CDs and cassettes.

Two months ago she ___ (be) at a concert together with some classmates.

The girls _____ (enjoy) the music there and had a lot of fun. But Kristy knows that school is more important than music at the moment.

IV. Using the language in different contexts

Defective dialogue: Questionnaire (18 p.)

In order to get some more information on "The truth about kids in Germany today", *The Guardian* has sent out questionnaires. Here is one for you to fill in. **Answer all the questions. Write about 80 words altogether. Count your words.**

What do you like best in your life?

_____
_____
_____

What are you interested in?

_____
_____
_____

What does music mean to you?

_____
_____
_____

Which media are important for you? Say why.

_____
_____
_____

What worries you?

_____
_____
_____

What ideas and hopes do you have for your future?

_____
_____
_____

V. Comment / Giving opinion

Write down your opinion on **one or two** of the following statements. (25 p.)

Give reasons for your opinion and/or examples. Write about 150 words altogether. Count your words.

- Violence on TV and in videos produces violence on the streets.
- School holidays are too long.
- Living in the city is better than living in the country.
- Being a teenager is the best time of your life.
- America – an example for Europe?

Lösung

I. Comprehension

1.

(1)	(2)	(3)	(4)	(5)	(6)
e	f	a	c	b	d

2. a) false   b) false
   c) false   d) true
   e) true   f) false
   g) false   h) false

II. Language

(1) their, (2) for, (3) away, (4) dream, (5) of having, (6) money, (7) selling, (8) to, (9) prison, (10) afraid, (11) different

III. Grammar

1.

noun	verb	adjective
activity/action	to act/to activate	active
hope	to hope	hopeful/hopeless
legality	to legalize	legal
respect	to respect	respectful/respectable

2. a) fit   b) more popular
   c) most important   d) more exciting
   e) laziest   f) more/much more
   g) less   h) serious

3. a) … they **will have** a good chance …
   (Hinweis: NS = Simple Present = HS = Simple Future)
   b) … if they **watched** less TV.
   (Hinweis: HS = could + infinitiv = NS = Simple Past))
   c) … young people **would not worry** if …
   (Hinweis: NS = Simple Past = HS = would + Infinitiv)

4. a) Who **offered (you) hash/in your school playground?**
   b) When **did/your friend/Steve/take hash/in your youth club?**
   c) Why **do you not take it?**
   d) Which drugs **have you already tried?**
   e) How **will you spend your pocket money/it/more sensibly?**

5. Antworten in folgender Reihenfolge:
   ... Kristy Lawson **is attending** Cranford High School
   (Hinweis: Signalwort = this year, Present Progressive)

   She **will finish** school ...
   (Hinweis: Signalwort = next term, Simple Future)

   The girl **has already applied** for ...
   (Hinweis: Signalwort = already, Simple Present Perfect)

   ... she **had**(Hinweis: Signalwort = last week, Simple Past)

   ... the firm **has not sent** her ...
   (Hinweis: Signalwort = yet, Simple Present Perfect)

   ... Kristy **works** hard for ...
   (Hinweis: Signalwort = every day, Simple Present)

   ... she **was** at a concert ...
   (Hinweis: Signalwort = two months ago, Simple Past)

   The girls **enjoyed** the music ...
   (Hinweis: Satz steht im Zusammenhang zum vorhergehenden = Simple Past)

IV. Using the language in different contexts

You: "In my life I like my family, my friends and my hobby best."

You: "I am interested in music. I play the guitar in our school band."

You: "Music is my favourite interest: I not only like listening to music but also making music."

You: "Television and the internet are very important for me because I not only get the latest information but also a lot of ideas for my homework and my hobby."

You: "It is very difficult to get an apprenticeship and this worries me. I am also afraid of the growing violence among young people."

You: "I hope to finish school successfully. Furthermore I will try to find an interesting job and of course I want to start a family in a few years."

V. Comment/Giving opinion

– **Violence on TV and in videos produces violence on the streets**
   It is a sad fact that violence on TV and in videos can cause aggression in real life. There are too many incidents every day which show that there is a connection between violence in films or TV-programmes and aggression on the streets.
   A lot of films with cruel and brutal scenes are lent to teenagers or even children in video-tape libraries. There are also too many violent programmes in the early evenings when children especially watch TV. Such programmes and films can have a strong effect on youngsters. They think violence and brutality are normal in human contact.

- **School holidays are too long**
  Probably, it will not be surprising that a student like me cannot agree with this statement.
  School, however, is hard work and that's why I need an appropriate amount of time for recreation. I do not get a lot of pocket money so I often take a summer holiday job in a super-market to earn some extra money. This money I spend on clothes, hobbies, leisure activities and things I cannot afford with my pocket money.
  I can understand parents who think that school holidays are too long because their children are only hanging around, but this need not be a problem.

- **Living in the city is better than living in the country.**
  Many young people think that living in the city is better than living in the country, and so do I. Therefore I can agree with this statement.
  A city has lots of entertainment and leisure facilities like theatres, cinemas, discotheques and stadiums. Young people can do different things there: going dancing, watching the latest movies or doing all kinds of sport and hobbies. Every day you can meet lots of interesting people there. Life does not seem to be boring in the city. On the other hand, I would say that living in the city does not only have advantages. Pollution, a great deal of traffic and noise are problems which make living in a city sometimes unpleasant.
  Therefore I can understand people who prefer living in the country.

- **Being a teenager is the best time of your life.**
  You often hear adults say that being a teenager is the best time of your life. I think we teenagers cannot only enjoy our lives but we face situations and things which are problematic for us as well. Therefore I only partly agree with this statement.
  What I like best about my life as a teenager is having understanding parents, friends and interesting hobbies. My mother and father show a lot of patience with me. I am happy to have a friend I can absolutely rely on. We share many interests and have a lot of fun together. Furthermore I enjoy the large variety of leisure facilities for young people. Nowadays it is hardly possible to be bored.
  In conclusion, I would say that being a teenager is a good time but far from being without its problems.

- **America – an example for Europe?**
  To my mind, this statement is put in too general a sense.
  Of course, there are things in America which the countries and people in Europe could take as an example, for instance the economic aspect that there is a lot of tax relief for firms and companies, so they are able to make and keep jobs.
  Furthermore I would mention the progressive opening hours. It is a great advantage to be able to go shopping at any time. But the fact that there is almost no social security system cannot be held up as a good example for our countries and their inhabitants.
  There is no doubt, that all countries and their people could learn from each other in different ways.

Useful words and phrases

to have an effect on sb.	– Auswirkung auf jmd. haben
to hang around	– herumhängen
tax relief	– Steuervergünstigungen
social security system	– Sozialversicherungssystem

Realschulabschluss Englisch in Mecklenburg-Vorpommern
Abschlussprüfung 2001: Listening Comprehension

What do you think of when you hear the words "summer holidays"? Probably sun and beaches, interesting spare time activities, travelling to foreign countries or sightseeing. You will find all this and even more in the following news.

Task A: Hard Rock Café

All over the world, Hard Rock Cafés are famous for hamburgers, guitars on the walls and loud music. Have you ever been in such a café? No? Well, then you should try a very special one.
It's the world's largest Hard Rock Café and it's in Orlando, Florida.
Since March 1999 it has got another great attraction: a huge concert hall next to the Café with live music. In fact, it's the only Hard Rock Café in the world that has live music so close. All its 2,500 seats were sold out when Elton John opened the hall in spring.
Music fans from all over the country have listened to music at the Hard Rock Café's concert hall since then.
From Monday to Thursday there's the Hard Rock Live Band. For $9 you can listen to a rock and roll concert with music from the past to the present. After the concert there's a live music show with surprise guests talking about the latest trends. At the weekend famous and not-so-famous new bands play.
But there is a lot more to see at the Hard Rock Café. If you go there, you must have a look at the 1958 Pink Cadillac over the bar. And don't miss the Café's collection of things that once belonged to famous people. There are clothes and musical instruments from stars like The Spice Girls, The Rolling Stones, Marilyn Manson, U2, Michael Jackson, and many more.

Task B: A Perfect Skateboarder

If you're a skateboarder, have you ever tried to jump and spin around on your board? Well, this summer, Tony Hawk was the first person in the world to spin two and a half times in the air! None of the people watching him could believe their eyes. What a great trick! Of course, Tony won the gold medal at this competition.
Later, a reporter asked Tony if he remembered his first time on a skateboard. And Tony told him, "Yeah, I was ten. My brother let me use his board behind our house. I went down in one direction. I didn't know how to turn around. Of course, I fell down and hurt my hands and knees. But I really wanted to learn skating. My brother helped me a lot and since then I've always trained hard. And I'm also trying new things on the ramp."
During the last twenty years Tony has worked to make skateboarding popular. "In the 90s," Tony remembers, "skateboarding nearly died out. People said that skateboarders were bad boys who always got into trouble."
But Tony's good example showed them that this was wrong. Young people admired him.
Tony is thirty now, and he is the oldest of the top skateboarders. He is married and has two children. And he owns a very successful skateboard company.
Tony is doing fewer competitions these days. He wants to spend more time with his family. But he thinks he's still too young to stop skateboarding.

Task C: Camping With the Fish

Imagine swimming deep under the sea. Blue, orange and pink fish are all around you. Look out for that big dangerous fish. It's a shark. It is swimming very slowly and looking very hungry. What a monster! And what are all these strange things moving in and out of the coral on the ocean floor? – You don't have to imagine. You can watch all the wonders of the deep sea from inside your own warm and dry sleeping bag. That's how some lucky kids from Northern California found out more about the Pacific Ocean – they camped out at the new Aquarium of the Pacific in Long Beach, California. 14-year-old Adam said, "Most of us are from small towns near Sacramento and we had a long drive to get down here. But it was really nice of the people to let us sleep overnight here. And now they are going to teach us everything about fish. I've never slept in an aquarium before, and I just hope these water tanks don't explode during the night."

Adam came to the aquarium along with about 20 other kids to learn about the Pacific Ocean. The kids' tour explored the three parts of the Aquarium which represent the big areas of the Pacific. As you know it's the world's largest body of water, covering almost half the earth. The programme at the aquarium combines science with sleep. The children really enjoyed the night when they went camping with the fish.

Task A: Hard Rock Café (6 p.)

Listen to the report and tick the correct information. There is only one answer per item.

1. In Hard Rock Cafés you will find
   - ☐ pictures on the walls.
   - ☐ loud music.
   - ☐ hot dogs.

2. In Orlando, Florida, there is the world's
   - ☐ craziest Hard Rock Café.
   - ☐ loudest Hard Rock Café.
   - ☐ biggest Hard Rock Café.

3. A Hard Rock Live Band plays live music
   - ☐ all week.
   - ☐ four days a week.
   - ☐ once a week.

4. Listening to a rock and roll concert costs
   - ☐ $19.
   - ☐ $9.
   - ☐ $90.

5. A live music show
   - ☐ surprises the guests.
   - ☐ has surprise guests.
   - ☐ is the latest trend.

6. The Café has collected
   - ☐ famous people.
   - ☐ stars.
   - ☐ musical instruments.

Task B: A Perfect Skateboarder

Try to find out if the following information is true or false. ☑ (7 p.)

	true	false
1. Tony Hawk was the first skateboarder in the world.	☐	☐
2. His brother was ten when Tony started skateboarding.	☐	☐
3. At his first try Tony was not very successful.	☐	☐
4. He learned the basics without anybody's help.	☐	☐
5. In the 90s only bad boys went skateboarding.	☐	☐
6. Today Tony has a successful business.	☐	☐
7. He hasn't given up skateboarding yet.	☐	☐

Task C: Camping With the Fish
There have been some errors during broadcasting. Correct them. (7 p.)

1 Imagine swimming deep under the sea. Brown, orange and pink fish are

2 all around you. Look out for that big dangerous fish, It's a shark. It is

3 swimming very lonely and looking very hungry. What a monster! And

4 what are all these strange things moving in and out of the coral on the

5 ocean floor? – You don't have to imagine. You can watch all the wonders

6 of the deep sea from inside your own warm and fine sleeping bag. That's

7 how some lucky kids from Northern California found out more about the

8 Pacific Ocean – they camped out at the new Aquarium of the Pacific in

9 Long Beach, California. 14-year-old Adam said, "Lots of us are from

10 small towns near Sacramento and we had a long drive to get down here.

11 But it was really nice of the people to let us sleep overnight here. And now

12 they are going to teach us everything about fish. I've never stepped in an

13 aquarium before, and I just hope these water tanks don't explode during

14 the night."

2001-4

15 Adam came to the aquarium along with about 30 other kids to learn about

16 the Pacific Ocean. The kids' tour explored the three parts of the Aquarium

17 which represent the big areas of the Pacific. As you know it's the world's

18 largest body of water, covering almost half the earth. The programme at

19 the aquarium combines science with sheep. The children really enjoyed

20 the night when they went camping with the fish.

Lösung

Task A

1 loud music
2 biggest Hard Rock Café
3 four days a week
4 $ 9
5 has surprise guests
6 musical instruments

Task B

1 false, 2 false, 3 true, 4 false, 5 false, 6 true, 7 true

Task C

	falsch	richtig
Zeile 1	brown	blue
Zeile 3	lonely	slowly
Zeile 6	fine	dry
Zeile 9	Lots	Most
Zeile 12	stepped	slept
Zeile 15	30	20
Zeile 19	sheep	sleep

> **Realschulabschluss Englisch in Mecklenburg-Vorpommern**
> **Abschlussprüfung 2001: Reading Comprehension**

The Californian Dream

People learn a lot from travelling. You see things which are interesting and enjoyable. You see some things in other countries which seem better than those in your own. There are other things from home which you miss and suddenly begin to appreciate. You learn to question your own culture and be more open-minded towards other cultures.
5 When you go to America you will find things which seem strange to non-Americans but which make sense as soon as you realize that Americans think that freedom is the most important thing in life.
And in which part of America is there more freedom than anywhere else? It has to be California. California gave birth to surfing – freedom on a high wave – and to the Walkman –
10 personal freedom of choice in music.
California was also the state from which freedom of information first exploded around the world on the Internet. There is no place in the USA that is as liberal as California towards people of a different creed[1], race or lifestyle. That's why the gay movement first started here.
15 California produced Disneyland, the home of Mickey Mouse, and Hollywood, the home of movies and movie stars. Millions of people escape every day from the real world into the artificial world of soap operas and computer games.
People originally came to California for gold. Today they come for their holidays. Many of them start with a visit to Disneyland, a place for children of all ages. At Disneyland you
20 can go on a boat journey through a tropical jungle; you can take a train through the American Wild West, travel in a spaceship, plunge into a pool at Splash Mountain … or just sit in the sun and eat ice-cream.
However, California is more than that. It's got beautiful scenery – mountains, forests and deserts. It has warm winters and hot summers, blue skies by day and wild parties on the
25 beach at night. That's the kind of freedom tourists are looking for.
But beware! Even California is not all fun. Your holiday enjoyment can easily turn to disappointment if you're not careful. As in other states and most parts of the world you can be offered drugs at any street-corner, and there are certain areas you'd better avoid if you don't want to risk being mugged.
30 American freedom has its down-side, you see, as it includes the freedom to carry guns. And one of the darker sides of the 'Sunshine State' is its crazy teenagers who can sometimes be found driving around, ramming cars and robbing tourists such as yourself.

1 creed: der Glaube

Aufgaben

I. Comprehension

1. Matching exercise. Combine the matching parts of the sentences: (6 p.)

   (1) Travel may help you
   (2) Americans love nothing more
   (3) Both the Walkman and surfing
   (4) Disneyland offers you the chance
   (5) Tourists enjoy
   (6) There are some crazy teenagers in California

   a) California's countryside, its climate and beach parties.
   b) to make some exciting journeys by different means of transport.
   c) who may rob tourists.
   d) than their own freedom.
   e) have their origins in California.
   f) to learn about other cultures.

(1)	(2)	(3)	(4)	(5)	(6)

2. True or false? Read the text carefully. Find out which statements are true and which are false. Mark with a cross. (8 p.)

	true	false
a) Travelling may teach you something about your own culture.	☐	☐
b) The Internet first started in California.	☐	☐
c) California is not very liberal to people of different races.	☐	☐
d) Today people still come to California to look for gold.	☐	☐
e) Only small children find lots to enjoy at Disneyland.	☐	☐
f) Drugs are not easily available in California.	☐	☐
g) People are allowed to carry guns in California.	☐	☐
h) Teenagers drive tourists around.	☐	☐

II. Language

1. Completion (11 p.)

   A friend of yours has gone to the United States for one year and is going to school there. This is an e-mail that you received a few days ago.

   to F@t-online.de   from PAT@schus.com

   Hi there,
   I'm really getting into the American way of life here. I've got used to school and my English is improving. Talking of English, I know your exams are getting close, so this time my mail is a test for you. It's to help you, of course. You have to fit some of the following words in the gaps to understand my letter. (But be careful, there are some left over.)
   Here goes!

   Your words: visited – their – movie – doesn't it – there – at – such – in – surf – clubs – pupils – often – ever – than

   My school here in California is really big. There are over two thousand (1) _____ who come from different countries. Many of them came from Mexico with their families because (2) _____ parents needed work. So a lot of them speak Spanish (3) _____ home. We have school in the afternoon but it's not so bad because we have more subjects (4) _____ in Germany. Some of them are different – (5) _____ as child-care and car mechanics.

   I'm doing car mechanics – it's real fun. After that there are lots of (6) _____ and activities like dancing, sports and cheerleader practice. California is great. We've (7) _____ Disneyland and we've been to some (8) _____ studios. The cowboy towns there don't look as real as in the films. Surfing here is exciting; the waves are really huge and if you're an expert you can (9) _____ for ages on a wave. I'm not an expert so I keep falling into the water. The beaches are fantastic, too. At the weekends we (10) _____ have parties on the beach.

   This life sounds better than in Germany, (11) _____? But it's not all good – but that's for the next mail. Let me have your answers to this test as soon as possible – you'll soon be an expert, too.

   Yours
   Pat

2. Using the dictionary (3 p.)

   The following words from the text have various meanings. Which of the meanings given in the dictionary is the one used in the text? Underline the best German translation.

   Text: *That's why the gay movement started there.*
   gay (line 13)

   | **gay** I *adj* **1.** lustig, fröhlich **2.** bunt, (farben)prächtig; fröhlich, lebhaft *(Farben)* | **3.** lebenslustig **4.** schwul *(homosexuell);* **5.** Schwulen ... **II** *s* Schwuler *m.* |

   Text: *That's the kind of freedom tourists are looking for.*
   kind (line 25)

   | **kind** I *s* Art, Sorte | **II** *adj* **1.** freundlich, liebenswürdig, nett (**to** zu): ~**to animals** tierlieb **2.** herzlich |

Text: *Your holiday enjoyment can easily turn to disappointment if you're not careful.*
turn (line 26)
turn I *s* **1.** (Um)Drehung **2.** Biegung, Kurve **make a right~** nach rechts abbiegen. **II** *v/t* **1.** drehen, *Schlüssel a.* herumdrehen **2.** verwandeln (**into** in) | **III** *v/i* **1.** sich drehen **2.** abbiegen; einbiegen (**onto** auf; **into** in) **3.** sich verwandeln (**into**, **to** in)

3. Using words of the same family (4 p.)

   Complete each sentence with the suitable word given below the sentence.

   a) In Silicon Valley technicians work on world-wide _____.
      communication / communicate / communicative

   b) The Californian life-style is a very _____ one.
      joy / enjoy / joyful

   c) Every week youngsters _____ on the streets of LA's poorer neighbourhoods.
      death / die / dead

   d) The huge Paramount Film Studios make a lasting _____ on every tourist.
      impression / impress / impressive

III. Using structures

1. Adverts at a travel agency (7 p.)

   You work at a travel agency. Your boss wants more people to book his trips. He has written down some ideas. Help him finish his adverts for San Francisco by using the method of comparison.

   a) Discover the unique charm of San Francisco Bay – all over the world it's as _____ (popular) as the city itself.

   b) You shouldn't miss a ride by cable car, this is the _____ (fascinating) way of sightseeing.

   c) At this giant fair children pay _____ (little) than adults.

   d) A walk along Fisherman's Wharf is surely _____ (interesting) than your daily soap.

   e) Near Pier 39 you'll find _____ (many) sea lions than you can imagine.

   f) Climb Telegraph Hill and you'll have the _____ (good) view of the city.

   g) In Chinatown you can try the _____ (wide) range of typical Asian food.

2. What if …? Write down your ideas completing the following sentences. (4 p.)
   a) If you never travel to other countries, _____

   b) The USA would be a safer place if _____

   c) If people hadn't found gold in California, _____

   d) My friends would be angry with me if _____

3. A verb-killer virus has destroyed all the correct forms of the verbs in the following computer text on immigrant life in California. Reconstruct the text. (8 p.)

   "I loved Vietnam, so leaving the country and all my friends made me very sad," says Nguyen Thinh. "But after the war life was very hard for me. Coming to the US was the best thing I could do."

   Mr Nguyen _____ (meet) his wife, Mai, on the boat to America in 1981. After he _____ (work) on a farm in Napa Valley, he wanted to _____ (try) something new and had different jobs in the area. Then the family moved to the city and he got a job in a laundry. Last year he _____ (fire) by his company.

   "Finding work these days _____ (be) hard because I don't speak English very well. All my friends are Vietnamese so I _____ often _____ (not talk) to Americans."

   Nguyen Mai works as an office cleaner. Their son, Scott, 14, is in high school and would _____ (like) to study math and computer science in college.

   "We hope our son _____ (have) a better future in this country," Mr. Nguyen says.

IV. Using the language in different contexts

1. Information gap task (6 p.)

   You have a lot more questions than the text on California could answer.

   What else would you like to know about California? Ask a travel agency 3 different kinds of question.

   a) _____

   b) _____

   c) _____

2. Questionnaire (8 p.)

A Canadian magazine wants to find out about some aspects of teenager life.

Please fill in the questionnaire in the magazine. Answer all the questions. Please give reasons for your answers. Write about 80 words altogether. Count your words.

a) Most teenagers use mobile phones today. Why do you think are they so popular?

b) You learn English at school. Where can you use it?

c) Which would you prefer to visit – the USA or Australia?

d) Why would you or wouldn't you buy things from the Internet?

e) What kinds of films or TV programmes do you watch?

f) Young Americans can get a car driving licence when they are 16. What do you think of this?

V. Comment/Giving opinion

Write down your opinion on **one or two** of the following statements. Give reasons for your opinion and/or examples. Write about 150 words altogether. Count your words. (25 p.)

- America – a magic word for teenagers.
- Travelling helps people understand each other.
- Youth crime is a problem not only in other countries.
- You don't need drugs to feel free or "high".
- Teenage problems and pleasures are the same all over the world.
- Having fun is the most important part of holidays.

Lösung

I. Comprehension

1.

(1)	(2)	(3)	(4)	(5)	(6)
f	d	e	b	a	c

2. a) true b) true
   c) false d) false
   e) false f) false
   g) true h) false

II. Language

1. (1) pupils, (2) their, (3) at, (4) than, (5) such, (6) clubs, (7) visited, (8) movie, (9) surf, (10) often, (11) doesn't it

2. gay:　　I 5　　Schwulen...
   kind:　　I　　　Art, Sorte
   turn:　　III 3　sich verwandeln

3. a) communication b) joyful
   c) die d) impression

III. Using structures

1. a) popular b) most fascinating
   c) less d) more interesting
   e) more f) best
   g) widest

2. a) ... you **won't/can't understand** people of different races and cultures.
   (Hinweis: Nebensatz = Simple Present; Hauptsatz = Simple Future)
   b) ... if there **were** stricter laws.
   (Hinweis: Hauptsatz = would + Inf; Nebensatz = Simple Past)
   c) ... this state **wouldn't have been** so attractive for settlers.
   (Hinweis: Nebensatz = Simple Past Perfect; Hauptsatz = would + have + been)
   d) ... if I **started smoking**.
   (Hinweis: Hauptsatz = would + Inf; Nebensatz = Simple Past)

3. Antworten in folgender Reihenfolge:

   Mr Nguyen **met** his wife ...
   (Hinweis: Signalwort = in 1981, Simple Past)
   After he **worked/had worked** on ... he wanted to **try** something ...
   (Hinweis: 1. Teilsatz steht im Zusammenhang mit dem 2. Teilsatz = Simple Past oder Simple Past Perfect; nach *to* folgt Infinitiv)
   ... he **was fired** by ...
   (Hinweis: Signalwort = last year, Simple Past, Passive Voice)
   ... these days **is** hard because ...
   (Hinweis: Signalwort = these days, Simple Present)
   ... so I **do not** often ...
   (Hinweis: allgemeingültige Aussage = Simple Present)
   ... and would **like** to study ...
   (Hinweis: nach would folgt immer der Infinitiv ohne *to*)
   ... our son **will have** a better future ...
   (Hinweis: Signalwort = hope, Simple Future)

IV. Using the language in different contexts

1. Mögliche Fragen könnten sein:

   a) What is the best time for travelling to California?

   b) Where are the most marvellous beaches there?

   c) I have already heard about several theme parks in California. Which could be interesting for me as a sports fan?

   d) I want to learn to surf during my stay in California. Can you recommend me a good but not so expensive surf-school?

2. Mögliche Antworten könnten sein:

   a) You: "Well, I think they are so popular because one can give somebody a call and can be called everywhere and at any time. That means a feeling of independence and security for people."

   b) You: "My English is not the best but I can use it every day when I surf the Internet. As my parents like travelling to foreign countries I also speak English during our stays there."

   c) You: "I have already been to the USA; therefore I would prefer to visit Australia. But Australia is also more interesting for me because of the rare animals and plants."

   d) You: "I wouldn't buy everything from the Internet but I would buy clothes because of the big variety of very trendy and fashionable ones."

   e) You: "My favourite TV programmes are sport – which I like watching at any time of the day. I especially like watching soccer on TV because I am a fan."

   f) You: "I think it is great. Driving a car makes you independent of public transport and you can organize your leisure time better. For me and my friends living in a village a driving licence at the age of 16 would be fantastic."

V. Comment / Giving opinion

- **America – a magic word for teenagers.**
  When you hear or read America you immediately think of the USA, and so do I. But America is not only a magic word for teenagers but also for everyone who thinks that the USA is synonymous with a country of limitless opportunities and freedom. Especially for teenagers the opportunity to get a driving licence at the age of 16 is very attractive.
  The United States mean adventure, a large variety of leisure facilities and the idea of dreams coming true for me and my friends. Therefore I would say America is the most magic word for teenagers at the moment.

- **Travelling helps people understand each other.**
  I fully agree with this statement because I think a trip to another country is the best opportunity to meet people and to learn about their culture, their traditions and their way of life.
  It is a sad fact that too many people in our country are prejudiced against foreigners. Therefore I would say only personal experience by travelling to other countries can break down prejudices.
  Finally, I am convinced that understanding each other across the borders is very important at a time of growing global problems.

- **Youth crime is not only a problem in other countries.**
  Generally speaking, youth crime is a very serious problem in our country. Especially in Mecklenburg Hither Pommerania the number of young people committing crimes has increased dramatically over the last few years.
  To my mind, one reason for this phenomenon is the growing youth unemployment in our area. Being out of work makes young people frustrated. They face problems they cannot solve.
  Although our government attaches great importance to prevention I think a useful way to prevent people from committing crime is to create and keep jobs for them.

- **You don't need drugs to feel free or "high".**
  I am firmly convinced that you don't need drugs to get in a good mood. I feel sorry for all young people who think that only taking Ecstasy, cocaine or grass can give them a feeling of freedom and satisfaction. Sometimes it seems to be normal that you can only have fun at parties for example by taking drugs. But I think that drugs are unnecessary and dangerous. Having fun and enjoying oneself is definitely possible without such harmful "measures". Reliable friends, understanding parents, sensible hobbies and success are more important for happiness and well-being in one's life than drugs.

- **Teenage problems and pleasures are the same all over the world.**
  Although I don't know teenagers in other countries personally, I suppose this statement is true. I don't doubt that everywhere teenagers like having friends and enjoying leisure time best. And I am sure teenagers' problems and worries are international as well. Problems with parents and friends, for example, or not having enough pocket money and looking for the right job are difficulties teenagers face every day all over the world irrespective of nationality and race.
  However, there are also parts of the world, in the poorest countries of Africa, for example, where young people do not have the chance to have a good time.

- **Having fun is the most important part of holidays.**
Probably, it will not be surprising that especially young people think that having a good time which includes fun is very important during the holidays, and so do I. Meeting friends, and going out as well as amusing myself by doing things which cannot be done at home are necessary for my recreation. But I can also understand that a lot of people like my parents have a different opinion about having fun and enjoying oneself.
That is why I have come to the conclusion that it depends on the people you are with whether having fun is the most important part of holidays or not.

Useful words and phrases

to be synonymous with   – gleichbedeutend sein mit
to be prejudiced against   – voreingenommen sein gegen
to have prejudices against   – Vorurteile haben gegen
to break down sth.   – etwas abbauen
to amuse oneself by doing   – sich die Zeit vertreiben mit

> **Realschulabschluss Englisch in Mecklenburg-Vorpommern**
> **Abschlussprüfung 2002: Hörverstehen**

When you think of your life as a teenager – what is it like?
Is it great parties? Hot fashion? Dangerous nights? Thrilling love?
Are there exciting sports? Colourful discos? Secret drugs? Shocking events?
You will now listen to three special reports for Channel 17.
This radio channel is airing the most exciting stories from your teenage world.

Task A: Rave to the grave

A rave party in East London nearly ended in tragedy last night. Over one hundred people were dancing in a flat when suddenly the floor broke. And all the dancers fell into the flat below.
Amazingly, no-one was killed. Only seven people were suffering from shock and had to be
5 taken to hospital.
David Goodyear was one of the ambulance men. He said that many of the party-goers hadn't even noticed the floor had collapsed. Most of the young people were so high on Ecstasy and other so-called 'dance drugs' that they just went on dancing.
Bert Jones, who is 64 years old, lives in the flat below. He said, "I must admit I hadn't
10 really noticed that there was a party going on. My hearing is very bad and I didn't have my hearing aid in, but I could feel the vibrations from somewhere. Then, suddenly there was a loud crash in the living room, so I ran in there. What I saw was terrible: the place was full of dust and plaster and people screaming. I just couldn't believe my eyes. I got the shock of my life, I can tell you."
15 Probably the extremely high volume of the techno music had shaken the floor too much, so that it broke.
This accident is not the first problem with techno parties all over London. More and more people are protesting against those parties and demanding stricter anti-rave laws. A spokesman for the Metropolitan Police said, "What worries us most is that where you have
20 rave parties, you have drugs, and where you have drugs you find organized crime."

Task B: Car Crazy

Lots of teenagers dream of the day they will be old enough to learn to drive and have their own car.
This is especially true of the average American teenager. When you ask them, most 16-year-old high school students will tell you that, yes, graduation and going on the college
5 are quite important for them right now.
But they will also tell you that passing their driving test and getting their license is the most important thing in their lives. Even their girlfriends come second.
If you want to know why, just look at the American way of life.
Only very few American city centres have public transport because Americans like to go
10 everywhere in their own cars. There are drive-in banks, drive-in movie theatres, drive-in restaurants and many other drive-ins.
Normally you can't even walk to the supermarket because there are no sidewalks.
This also means when young people want to meet their friends someplace they also have to ask their parents to take them. And, of course, after the party it's not so nice when your
15 parents have to pick you up again.
American teenagers can only feel free and independent when they are allowed to drive themselves. And, of course, having their own car is their biggest wish. This means that they are adults at last. They can go out where they like, when they like and with whom they like without asking any grown-ups.

Task C: Thrillseekers

'Soft adventure' has become a new form of holiday experience. The activities that travel agencies are offering go from whitewater rafting to climbing some of the world's highest mountains. But for some people this is not exciting enough. They want to take part in extreme sports.
5 The main attraction of these sports is that they are risky. People who do them might be injured or even die.
Take 'base jumping', for example, that's parachuting from cliffs and tall buildings. In the USA it's forbidden. And when you look at the statistics you'll know why: one in 700 base jumps ends in a death. This compares to only one in 90.000 for traditional parachuting.
10 Another extremely dangerous sport is 'absolute diving'. That's diving while you hold your breath – and a big weight. The world record is 417 feet.
Why is it that more and more people want to experience danger?
Brendan Koerner, a Washington journalist who has written many articles about extreme sports, explains that the popularity of extreme sports in America is a reaction against the
15 comfortable life many people live there. There are lots of little rules in American life that try to make it as safe as possible. This goes against the American sense of adventure.
"Look at all those Hollywood movies, there are all sorts of action stars. And in real life adventure freaks are asking, 'Where is my thrill?'"

Aufgaben

Task A: Rave to the Grave

Listen to the report and tick the correct information. There is only **one** answer per item. (6 p.)

1. More than a hundred people
   - [ ] crashed through a floor.
   - [ ] were killed.
   - [ ] went to hospital.

2. After the fall many young people
   - [ ] collapsed.
   - [ ] didn't stop dancing.
   - [ ] had taken Ecstasy.

3. Bert Jones
   - [ ] went to a rave party.
   - [ ] is 46 years old.
   - [ ] has a hearing aid.

4. Mr Jones couldn't
   - [ ] see very well.
   - [ ] feel the shaking of the floor.
   - [ ] hear properly.

5. People in London
   - [ ] are against anti-rave laws.
   - [ ] complain about rave parties.
   - [ ] love techno parties.

6. Drugs at rave parties
   - [ ] are connected with organized crime.
   - [ ] don't worry the police.
   - [ ] are worrying for criminals.

Task B: Car Crazy

Try to find out if the following information is true or false. (7 p.)

	true	false
1. Many teenagers dream of owning a car.	☐	☐
2. For most 16-year-old high school students cars are more important than their girlfriends.	☐	☐
3. There's not much public transport in many American cities.	☐	☐
4. In the USA you can go to many places without leaving your car	☐	☐
5. Usually you can't work in supermarkets.	☐	☐
6. Young people are glad when their parents fetch them from the party.	☐	☐
7. Driving themselves is a sign of independence for American teenagers.	☐	☐

Task C: Thrillseekers

There have been some errors during broadcasting. Correct them. (7 p.)

1 'Soft adventure' has become a new form of holiday experience. The

2 activities that travel agencies are offering go from whitewater rafting to

3 climbing some of the world's finest mountains. But for some people this

4 is not exciting enough. They want to take part in extreme sports. The main

5 attraction of these sports is that they are misty. People who do them might

6 be injured or even die. Take 'base jumping', for example, that's

7 parachuting from cliffs and tall buildings. In the USA it's forbidden. And

8 when you look at the statistics you'll know why: one in 1,700 base jumps ends

9 in a death. This compares to only one in 90,000 for traditional parachuting.

10 parachuting. Another extremely dangerous sport is 'absolute diving'.

11 That's diving while you hold your breath – and a big weight. The world

12 record is 417 feet. Why is it that more and more people want to experience

13 changes? Bernard Koerner, a Washington journalist who has read many

14 articles about extreme sports, explains that the popularity of extreme

15 sports in America is a reaction against the comfortable life many people

16 live there. There are lots of little schools in American life that try to make

17 it as safe as possible. This goes against the American sense of adventure.

18 "Look at all that Hollywood movies, there are all kinds of action stars.

19 And in real life adventure freaks are asking, 'Where is my thrill?'"

Lösung

Task A

1 crashed through a floor
2 didn't stop dancing
3 has a hearing aid
4 hear properly
5 complain about rave parties
6 are connected with organized crime

Task B

1 true, 2 true, 3 true, 4 true, 5 false, 6 false, 7 true

Task C

	falsch	richtig
Zeile 3	finest	highest
Zeile 5	misty	risky
Zeile 8	1700	700
Zeile 13	changes	danger
Zeile 13	read	written
Zeile 16	schools	rules
Zeile 18	kinds	sorts

> Realschulabschluss Englisch in Mecklenburg-Vorpommern
> Abschlussprüfung 2002: Reading Comprehension

Living Clean – Living Cool?

Most of them don't look like mama's darlings. Some of them have pierced tongues. Others are proud of their tattoos. But how these teenagers live – and what they think – is a conservative parent's dream: no drugs, no cigarettes, no alcohol, no sex before marriage. What's this? Are we talking about ugly outsiders who are left alone in the schoolyard
5 because no-one likes them? Not at all. We are talking about "straight edge[1] teens". More and more teenagers are proud of living a clean life – not only in the USA.
I'm a person just like you,
but I've got better things to do
than sit around and smoke dope ...
10 *I've got a straight edge.*
Twelve years ago, these lines from a song by the band Minor Threat made the words "straight edge" famous. The band's singer Ian MacKaye knew what he was singing about: a good friend of his had died from an overdose.
Today, the idea of being "straight edge" is stronger than ever.
15 "Just because I don't use drugs doesn't mean I'm not cool", Jeremy Smith of Tacoma, Washington, told **Spot on**[2]. Many thousands of miles east of Washington, in Bodö, Norway, Fredrik Bakkemo quotes another line by Minor Threat. "I don't drink, I don't smoke, I don't sleep around." And he adds: "I just want to be a good example to other people." Jeremy and Fredrik both know the other side of life. "For me and my friends drinking
20 alcohol at our parties was normal", says Fredrik, "I didn't even like the feeling of being drunk."
Jeremy's life was dealing in sex and cocaine until his best friend died of AIDS at the age of 17. Jeremy remembered the message behind the Minor Threat songs – and decided to live "straight edge".
25 There isn't one single definition of living "straight edge". It can mean a lot of different lifestyles.
Many "straight edgers" are vegetarians and don't eat meat. Some of them, called vegans, don't even use any kind of animal products like eggs or milk. Others say no to alcohol, nicotine, coffee or even chocolate. Many are surfers or skaters or do other sorts of sports.
30 They feel that their sport gives them enough of a kick so that they can do without drugs. "When I had my health check-up for football, the doctor asked me, 'Do you drink, do you smoke, do you take drugs?' I said no – and felt good", says Chris Reagan, from Los Gatos, California.
Living this way does not mean that Jeremy, Fredrik and all the other "straight edgers" have
35 become bores[3] or couch potatoes. Of course not. These people lead very active lives. For most of them keeping fit and healthy is as important as having fun. "But we know the risks. We love to party hard, but safe," Nora Mountford, 17, from Santa Clara, California, explained.
Whatever is most important to a "straight edge" teenager, they all seem to agree on one
40 thing. "Straight edge living", says Nora, "is about being happy with yourself and for us this means: living clean is cool."

adapted from Spot on 21–22/2000

1 straight edge – (wörtlich: gerade Kante) hier etwa: moralisch/ethisch konsequent
2 Spot on – Das Junior-Magazin von Spotlight
3 bores – Langweiler

Aufgaben

I. Comprehension

1. Matching exercise. Combine the matching parts of the sentences: (6 p.)

   (1) Conservative parents
   (2) Ian MacKaye
   (3) Frederik Bakkemo
   (4) The death of Jeremy's best friend
   (5) Straight edgers
   (6) Jeremy, Frederik and other straight edgers

   a) lost a good friend to a drug overdose.
   b) find sports an adequate substitute for drugs
   c) are pleased with the way straight edge teenagers live.
   d) do not lead boring lives.
   e) wants to be a good role model for others.
   f) helped him change his life.

(1)	(2)	(3)	(4)	(5)	(6)

2. Read the text carefully. Find out which statements are true and which are false. Mark with a cross. (8 p.)

   true false

   a) Straight edge teens are lonely outsiders whom nobody likes ☐ ☐
   b) The words "straight edge" became popular through a song by Minor Threat. ☐ ☐
   c) Jeremy was 17 when his best friend died. ☐ ☐
   d) Vegans are a special type of vegetarians. ☐ ☐
   e) Some straight edgers don't even allow themselves chocolate. ☐ ☐
   f) The doctor asked Chris if he took drugs. ☐ ☐
   g) Straight edgers prefer keeping fit and healthy to having fun. ☐ ☐
   h) Nora is a straight edge teenager. ☐ ☐

II. Language

1. Completition (11 p.)

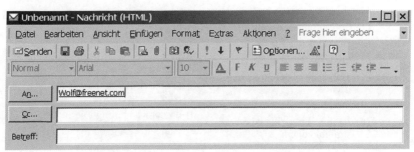

Hi Wolfgang,
Learning for our English exam can be boring alone. So I thought it would be a good idea to make some tests for each other. Just take any text and shift about 10 words and add about 5 more, then mail it to me. Here's one for you. See if you can solve it.

Your words:
matter – been – dream – without – unhealthy – keen – an – until – arrived – think – a – those – vegetarian – imagine – by – stuff

I've just read (1) _____ article about people who seem to be health freaks. They don't drink alcohol or coffee, don't smoke and don't eat meat or chocolate – and sex is taboo (2) _____ they get married! I don't know if I could live like that. Well, I like sports, too. I play volleyball, I'm in a football team and I love swimming and cycling in the summer; but I don't think I could do (3) _____ all those things.
Can you (4) _____ a party without alcohol?
I don't (5) _____ you have to drink a lot but I've never (6) _____ to a party where there was no alcohol. I'm not so (7) _____ on meat, so I could become a (8) _____, but I couldn't survive without chocolate.
Lots of girls at school have piercings. I think that's a (9) _____ of taste but perhaps a pierced tongue or other piercings in your mouth could be (10) _____. What about you? Do you think you could live without all (11) _____ things?
Yours
Joachim

2. Using the dictionary (3 p.)

The following words from the text have various meanings. Which of the meanings given in the dictionary is the one used in the text? Underline the best German translation.

Text: ... *I've got better things to do than sit around and smoke dope* ...

dope (line ??)

| **dope I** s **1.** Stoff *(Rauschgift)* **2.** Dopingmittel *(Sport)* **3.** *(sl.)* Trottel | **II** *v/t* **1.** *j-m* Stoff geben **2.** dopen *(Sport)* **3.** ein Betäubungsmittel untermischen |

Text: *Jeremy's life was in dealing sex and cocaine until his best friend died of AIDS at the age of 17.*

deal (line ??)

| **deal I** s **1.** Menge, **a great ~** sehr viel **2.** Geschäft, Handel **II** *v/i (irr)* **1. ~ with** sich befassen *od.* beschäftigen mit **2. ~ with** behandeln *od.* zum Thema haben | **III** *v/t* **1. ~** Handel treiben *od.* Geschäfte machen mit **2.** *(Kartenspiel)* geben **3. ~ out** austeilen, verteilen |

Text: *We love to party hard, but safe,* ...

party (line ??)

| **party I** s **1.** *pol.* Partei, **within the ~** innerparteilich **2.** Gesellschaft, Gruppe: **we were** | **a ~ of three** wir waren zu dritt **3.** Gesellschaft, Party, Fest **II** *v/r* feiern, eine Party machen |

3. Using words of the same family. Complete each sentence with the suitable word given below the sentence. (4 p.)

a) At many parties music and fun _____ a cool atmosphere.
   (creation – create – creative)

b) Sometimes junkies _____ that they risk their lives.
   (realization – realize – real)

c) Today _____ treatment can help addicts to keep away from drugs.
   (speciality – specialize – special)

d) Teenage _____ has been normal in all generations.
   (rebellion – rebel – rebellious)

III. Using structures

1. Lately, I found the following summer quiz of a travel agency in my mail: (7 p.)

"You don't know how to spend your holiday? If you fill in this form correctly and compare some details, you will get a choice of thrilling adventures and might even win one of them."

Enjoy rushing down the mountains on your board. You'll be _____ (fast) than a bird.
Experience the world upside down. For your first bungee jump you need _____ (little) courage than you think.
You hate a _____ (boring) summer? So you should try wakeboarding and learn the _____ (crazy) tricks you've ever heard of.

Your video game isn't as _____ (fascinating) as our rafting tour. Come and join our crew.
Sharks? Many people are afraid of them. You needn't be. While diving with us you'll discover the _____ (attractive) underwater mysteries in the world.
Are you looking for the _____ (good) excitement in your holiday? Do parachuting and jump into the clouds.

2. What if …? Write down your ideas completing the following sentences. (4 p.)

   a) If I did bungee jumping, _____
   _____

   b) If Chris had taken drugs, _____
   _____

   c) If you offer meat to a vegetarian, _____
   _____

   d) I would be extremely happy if _____
   _____

3. German football fans were shocked and couldn't understand why Germany's most talented footballers were going to play for English teams. (8 p.)

   The latest edition of KICK, a popular football magazine, came up with the following task for its readers to find out for themselves. They just had to complete a text about one of them, Thomas Witzelsperger. **Can you do it, too?**
   In August 2000 Thomas _____ (sign) a two-year professional contract with Aston Villa-Birmingham. Before he _____ (go) to Birmingham he _____ (play) for Bayern Munich. When Thomas was asked why he left Bayern Munich he answered, "It's harder at Bayern Munich to _____ (get) into the first team. Nowadays the managers _____ (buy) foreign players and internationals, so a young player _____ (have) no chance."
   Thomas _____ already _____ (taste) first-team football in Birmingham. He came on as a substitute for ten minutes against Liverpool. All his friends hope he _____ (get) more chances to play for the first team at the end of the season.
   But Thomas still dreams of becoming a star for FC Bayern.

IV. Using the language in different contexts

1. Information gap task. You have a lot more questions than the text *Living clean – living cool?* could answer. (6 p.)

   What else would you like to ask the people in the text about living straight edge? Ask 3 different kinds of questions that haven't been answered yet.

   a) _____
   _____

   b) _____
   _____

   c) _____
   _____

2. Questionnaire (18 p.)

An American magazine wants to find out about some aspects of European teenagers' lives.

Please fill in the questionnaire in the magazine. Answer all the questions. Please give reasons for your answers. Write at least 80 words altogether. Count your words.

a) How can you spend your free time in your area?

b) Name a few things that make your life pleasant.

c) How would you react if your best friend took drugs at a party?

d) In which way do the media influence your life?

e) What does the term "future" mean to you?

f) To what extent do the present day events in the world concern you?

V. Comment/Giving opinion

Write down your opinion on **one** of the following statements.
Give reasons for your opinion using examples where possible. Write about 150 words altogether. Count your words.

(25 p.)

- Driving after the disco can ruin lives.
- Surfing the Internet in your spare time has pros and cons.
- TV is the most useful spare time activity for youngsters.
- Telephones are a pleasure and a curse.
- There's no proper party without the right music and lots of alcohol.
- These days are not the time for fun and parties.
- Having a role model is good for young people.

Lösung

I. Comprehension

1.

(1)	(2)	(3)	(4)	(5)	(6)
c	a	e	f	b	d

2. a) false   b) true
   c) false   d) true
   e) true   f) true
   g) false   h) true

II. Language

1. (1) an, (2) until, (3) without, (4) imagine, (5) think, (6) been, (7) keen, (8) vegetarian, (9) matter, (10) unhealthy, (11) those

2. dope: I 1   Stoff (Rauschgift)
   deal: III 1 Handel treiben oder Geschäfte machen mit
   party: II   feiern, eine Party machen

3. a) create   b) realize
   c) special   d) rebellion

III. Using structures

1. faster, less, boring, craziest, fascinating, most attractive, best

2. a) ... I would be very excited.
   (Hinweis: Nebensatz = Simple Past, Hauptsatz = would + Inf.)
   b) ... he would not have been so fit.
   (Hinweis: Nebensatz = Simple Past Perfect, Hauptsatz = would + have + been)
   c) ... he/she will probably refuse.
   (Hinweis: Nebensatz = Simple Present, Hauptsatz = Simple Future)
   d) ... if I was in New York for a few months.
   (Hinweis: Hauptsatz = would + Inf., Nebensatz = Simple Past)

3. ... Thomas **signed** a two-year ...
   (Hinweis: Signalwort = in August 2000, Simple Past)
   ... he **went** to ... he **had played** for ...
   (Hinweis: Signalwort = before, Simple Past, 2. Teilsatz steht mit 1. Teilsatz im Zusammenhang = Simple Past Perfect)
   ... at Bayern Munich to **get** into ...
   (Hinweis: nach to folgt Infinitiv)
   ... the managers **buy** foreign players ... a young player **has** no chance.
   (Hinweis: Signalwort = nowadays, Simple Present, beide Teilsätze stehen im Zusammenhang)
   Thomas **has** already **tasted** first-team ...
   (Hinweis: Signalwort = already, Simple Present Perfect)
   ... he **will get** more chances ...
   (Hinweis: Signalwort = hope, Simple Future oder Simple Present)

IV. Using the language in different contexts

1. a) Do you often try to convince people to become "straight edgers"?
   b) What sorts of sports do you prefer?
   c) Why is the idea of being "straight edge" not popular in Europe yet?

2. a) My area offers a lot of free time facilities. There are several clubs, such as online cafés, cinemas, discotheques and a lot of sports centres. My friends and I love sports, so we often go to the sports centre near our school.
   b) I enjoy my life. My family, friends and my hobbies make it pleasant and interesting. I have understanding and tolerant parents who give me enough pocket money so I can afford to buy CDs, tickets for the cinema and much more. My friends are reliable and we share a lot of interests.
   c) First I would be shocked but then I would try to talk to him/her in order to find out his/her reasons. Of course, I would try to convince him/her that drugs are dangerous and that he/she must stop taking them.
   d) Well, I must admit that media do influence my life. Advertisements on TV, especially, make me buy several products. But I would say that media do not have a strong effect on me and my opinion because I can tell the difference between reality and the world shown in the media.

e) To me, the future means becoming independent from my parents. Furthermore, the term future is very close connected with my desire for a successful professional career. Finally, it also means starting my own family.

f) The current day events worry me. It is very hard to be carefree nowadays. But I also think we must all look forward because there is a lot of good news and good things happening everywhere as well.

V. Comment/Giving opinion

Hinweis: In dieser Aufgabe sollst du dich mit einem von dir gewählten Statement (Behauptung, Feststellung) auseinandersetzen. Formuliere deine Meinung, begründe diese und versuche, Beispiele u. a. aus deinem Erfahrungsbereich heranzuziehen. Versuche deine schriftlichen Äußerungen logisch zu gliedern und auf die bereits bekannten Wendungen zurückzugreifen.

– **Driving after the disco can ruin lives.**
Unfortunately, I have to agree with this statement. In Mecklenburg Hither Pommerania it has been sad reality for the last few years that driving after the disco can ruin lives. There are more casualties in accidents after discos in our country than at any other place in Germany. Woodned crosses along several highways are silent witnesses to this dramatic situation. But what are the reasons for so many accidents happening after discos? First, I would say that too many young drivers overrate their driving experience and their reactions. They drive too fast and take too many risks. Another serious problem is drinking and driving. Almost every second "disco accident" happens under the influence of alcohol. What can be done to prevent drivers from drinking? To my mind, it is necessary to increase police controls in car-parks in front of the discotheques. Drunk drivers must be stopped from using their cars. Besides, I am convinced that friends can make a difference, too. For example, when my friends and I go to the disco we make sure that the driver does not drink alcohol, although I have to admit that we only became aware of this problem after the sister of a friend was very badly injured in a car crash after a disco. The driver was drunk and speeding. To sum up, I would say all disco-goers could prevent such dramatic accidents if they used the fifty-fifty ticket for public transport and taxis.

– **Surfing the Internet in your spare time has pros and cons.**
Surfing the Internet is my favourite spare time activity, which is why I have chosen this statement. It is true that there are pros and cons but I think that there are more advantages than disadvantages. First, I am convinced that the Internet is one of the greatest inventions of our time. This enormous databank is an unlimited source of information. You can expand your knowledge on all aspects of life, history, science and so on. Since I have been using the net, doing homework and preparing for lessons has got easier for me because I can find all the answers to my questions very quickly. Furthermore, I think the service offered by the Internet has made our life more convenient. Without leaving your front door you can do shopping, or can book tickets or trips at any time. So the net is very timesaving, as well. Moreover, the Internet is a place to "meet" other people. I have already chatted to people living all over Europe. On the other hand, there are disadvantages, too. Acquiring information and using the services offered in the Internet can be very expensive. Sometimes there are providers trying to pull a fast one on you, so you have to be very careful. Besides, it is a sad fact that the net is often misused for criminal activities like the distribution of pornography. However, in conclusion, I would say that the Internet has opened up a new world for us which must be handled with care and responsibility.

- TV is the most useful spare time activity for youngsters.
TV can be a useful spare time activity for youngsters but it is not the most useful one. Therefore I can only partly agree with this statement. TV has become a central part of many people's lives because audiovisual impressions are easily received. Watching TV can be very informative, not only for young people. There are a lot of programmes with a high standard of education to expand childrens' knowledge, for example. However, more and more you can see children sitting in front of the TV set in their spare time instead of spending time with friends or playing outside. Furthermore, too many violent programmes are broadcast at times when youngsters usually watch TV. Cartoons or science fiction films are sometimes full of violent scenes. Children are easily influenced and think there is no difference between TV and real life. Therefore I would say that reading books, meeting friends, doing sports, discovering nature or simply playing are more useful spare time activities than watching TV.

- Telephones are a pleasure and a curse.
In my opinion the invention of the telephone by Alexander Bell was a breakthrough of that time. It made life easier and safer. Therefore I can only partly agree with the statement. I would say that telephones are more a pleasure than a curse. It depends on you whether the telephone is a useful machine or an accursed thing that causes stress. With the help of the telephone you can call everybody everywhere and at any time. Information can be transported very fast. That is not only useful in everyday life but for business as well. There is hardly a field in business today which does not use a telephone and I do not know a single person who does without it. It is hard to imagine what life was like without telephones. In emergencies or serious situations especially, a telephone can be a great help. Furthermore, I think the telephone makes life more convenient because it is timesaving. There is a large variety of services you can use by telephone, so you save a lot of time that you can spend on doing other important things. I expect my parents would say the telephone is a curse because calling my friends takes a lot of time and is expensive, too. But I am convinced that my parents agree with me that the telephone is an important, useful, timesaving and convenient device.

- There's no proper party without the right music and lots of alcohol.
My friends and I like parties, which is why I have chosen this statement. But I do not think that lots of alcohol is necessary for a proper party. It seems to be normal that it is not a party without a lot of beer or wine. Guests are always encouraged to drink, irrespective of age. One can only be in a good mood under the influence of alcohol. This is a widely heard opinion. Drinking alcohol seems to be harmless. I feel sorry for everyone who thinks that you can only have fun at a party if you drink a lot of alcohol, for example. To my mind, alcohol drunk in moderation can help you to relax but it depends on the person. However, in my opinion enjoying a party is definitely impossible without good music. A proper mixture of several sorts of music is a must for every party. Finally, I would say the latest music, funny games, interesting people, a relaxed atmosphere and alcohol taken in moderation can provide great entertainment for a proper party.

- These days are not the time for fun and parties.
I think it is very hard to be carefree at the moment because of the terrible and tragic incidents in our country. I was shocked when I heard what had happened in a grammar school in Erfurt. My classmates and I have had discussions for weeks on the question of who or what is to blame for this worrying situation. We could not find a reasonable answer, but we think that doing without fun and parties cannot be a solution and is definitely not the right way to prevent such incidents. Therefore I do not agree with the above-mentioned statement. To my mind, this crime shows that

violence on the screen can cause aggression and violence in real life. I am convinced that violent computer-games can have a strong effect on youngsters but they are not the only cause for the increasing violence in schools, for example. These days we face the fact that we all have to be more active and show more commitment in order to be able to prevent violence and aggression in everyday life. Personally, I have come to the conclusion that people mind their own business too often instead of paying attention to each other. To sum up, I would stress that it is necessary to look forward. Taking a critical look at the problems of violence and aggression does not mean stopping enjoying life.

- **Having a role model is good for young people.**
I cannot fully agree with this statement. A lot of youngsters have role models, such as singers, actors, sportsmen and entertainers. Young people worship them because of their appearance or manner. However, I do not think that emulating stars makes sense because you cannot learn the really important things in life from them. To my mind, young people need a good example to be set by grown-ups in general. I do not think emulating a special person is necessary if you have a family and friends. My parents are the most important people in my life because they give me love and security. They teach me abilities and qualities which I will need when I become independent from them. Learning by experience, and learning strategies, methods and skills for your life is more important than having a special role model. I have come to the conclusion that the people around you have a more significant meaning for you and a much greater effect on you than role models can have.

Useful words and phrases
casualties	– Verletzte, Tote
to drink alcohol in moderation	– Alkohol in Maßen trinken
to emulate sb.	– jmdm. nacheifern

> **Realschulabschluss Englisch in Mecklenburg-Vorpommern**
> **Abschlussprüfung 2003: Hörverstehen**

The media are all around us every day. TV and radio stations bring good and bad news into our homes. Newspapers and magazines tell about everyday life as well as the latest events and gossip about the famous and the rich. Mobile phones and the Internet get you connected to the world in no time. Call Centres boom and chatrooms are the new playground for the younger generation.

Here are some stories from the world of the media.

Task A: Sorry, I'm Bob

Have you ever heard of the Royal Prince Harry, the most famous 18-year-old in the world? These days you can read lots of stories about him in the British press. The journalists especially like to report on dangers and adventures in Harry's life.

And Harry loves dangerous sports! When he and his brother William climbed down a cliff
5 on a rope without helmets, the British newspapers went crazy because of the risks. It's not every day that you see the future king and his brother going over a cliff like that!

But Harry also has a gentle side. Britain loved him and William when they stopped to help a driver with his broken-down car. "It was no big deal," the royal boys said. But the owner of the car didn't agree. "It's amazing when two princes push your car down the street," he
10 said.

What else are the papers writing about? For instance Harry's wild side. Over the past years, he's been in trouble for smoking cannabis, drinking alcohol and driving without a seatbelt! When he wanted to be year representative at his famous school, Eton, his schoolmates didn't think he was right for the job. Why? "Harry is popular but his behaviour is
15 not the best," said one of his schoolmates.

Harry is no longer the shy little boy who used to hide behind his brother in public. At the Queen's Jubilee last year, the world saw a confident young man. He was even waving to the crowd of fans and singing along with the music. But when Harry goes out in private he still hides his face behind a baseball cap and dark sunglasses. What does he do if fans rec-
20 ognise him? "I just say, 'Sorry, I'm Bob!'", the young prince laughs.

Harry is busy planning for his future. He loves art and wants to study it at university just like his brother. And he already has a girlfriend. Millions of girls will be sad to hear that Harry is in love with 20-year-old Nicola Sturgis – his next-door neighbour at his home, Highgrove. – Another story for the greedy media ...

Task B: Snowball e-mails

Have you ever forwarded an e-mail? You surely know what it means: to forward an e-mail. It means you get an interesting or important mail from someone and you send it on to somebody else. That's what I learnt in school. It's easy.

I'm Linda Griffith from North Carolina. Not long ago some students at a school in Los
5 Angeles, California, asked pupils from our school to forward an interesting e-mail. They wrote: "We are trying to see which places in the world an e-mail can travel in six weeks. Please, answer with the name of your country and then forward the e-mail to everyone you know."

That sounded to me like a great way to meet a lot of people from other countries. I wrote
10 an e-mail in English, sent it to everyone I knew and then asked them to forward it to eve-

2003-1

ryone they knew. So I waited to see how many answers I got. I thought it was a good idea: lots of contacts around the world, lots of surprises – and in the end I could choose which person I wanted to write back to.
But sadly, it didn't work. The Internet is simply too powerful! It reaches too many people
15 too quickly.
Our school got more than 500,000 e-mails in one month – that's over 1,600 every day! Nobody was able to read them all, let alone answer them!
Funnily enough, we also heard this on the radio about the Taonul School in New Zealand. They had to stop a similar project after only a few days. The school's e-mail address got
20 overloaded and people started phoning to say that they couldn't send their e-mails. The school's headmaster said, "I would be crazy if I tried the project again".
And I think he is right.

Task C: Britstyle Films

"Hello, my name, you want to know my name. It's Dave Williams. I'll say it again, Dave Williams.
My address is 4, Old London Road, Manford. CF2 3RT. Yes, I can repeat that …
4, Old London Road, Manford. I'll spell that M-A-N-F-O-R-D.
5 And the post code is C-F-2-3-R-T … C-F-2-3-R-T
My age – I'm 16 years old.
My favourite star – well that's not easy – I like so many; I think it's … Bruce Lee.
Yes, Bruce Lee, he's really cool.
My favourite film. That's an easy one. I like Star Wars 3. And you want to know what my
10 favourite type of film is. That's easy, too. I like action films. Action films with lots of fighting and loud music.
How often I go to the cinema. That's not so easy 'cos I watch most films at home on video, but I suppose I go to the cinema 4 times a year. No, not more than that. Yes, 4 times a year.
15 And who do I go with? Well, that's a very personal question. All I'll say is that I go with a good friend. I don't want to say any more than 'a good friend'.
That's all fine. What did you say? You'll send me a voucher to visit your studios? Great! Can I bring my friend?"

Aufgaben

Task A: Sorry, I'm Bob

Listen to the report and tick the correct information. There is only **one** answer per item. (7 p.)

1. Harry and William got down a cliff
   - [ ] and didn't wear helmets.
   - [ ] with helmets.
   - [ ] without dangerous risks.

2. William and Harry helped a driver
   - [ ] who had broken down.
   - [ ] who had pushed the car down the street.
   - [ ] whose car had broken down.

3. Harry's schoolmates
- [ ] wanted him to be year representative[1] at Eton.
- [ ] didn't want him to be year representative.
- [ ] liked smoking cannabis.

4. Today Harry
- [ ] is a shy little boy.
- [ ] often hides behind William in public.
- [ ] waves to his fans and sings with the music.

5. If fans recognise him when he goes out in private
- [ ] he says he is Bob.
- [ ] he wears dark sunglasses.
- [ ] he plays baseball.

6. Harry wants to
- [ ] study the same subject as his brother.
- [ ] plan his future with his brother.
- [ ] be busy at university.

7. Harry is in love with
- [ ] millions of girls.
- [ ] Nicola Sturgis.
- [ ] a sad close friend.

[1] year representative – Jahrgangssprecher

Task B: Snowball e-mails

Try to find out if the following information is true or false.   (7 p.)

true false

1. "To forward" an e-mail means: you get an e-mail and send it on to someone else.
2. You can't learn at school how to forward an e-mail.
3. Pupils at a Californian school wanted to find out where and how far an e-mail could get in six weeks.
4. Linda asked all the people she knew to forward her e-mail to people they knew.
5. The idea didn't work because too many e-mails arrived in a very short time.
6. Linda's school got 50,000 e-mails in four weeks.
7. Taonul School's headmaster doesn't want to try the project again.

Task C: Britstyle Films

A British film company wants to find out which kinds of films and videos their audiences like best. They phone up young people to find out.

You will now hear the answers that one young man gave. Please fill in the information in the questionnaire below so that your company gets all the information they want to have. (6 p.)

BRITSTYLE FILMS
LIFE AND STYLE VIDEOS AND FILMS

Name: _____ Dave _____ Williams.

Address: _____

1 _____

2 Favourite British or American film star:
   _____

3 Favourite type of film:
   _____

4 Why favourite film?
   _____

5 How often do you go to the cinema?
   _____

6 Who do you go with?
   _____

Lösung

Task A

1. and didn't wear helmets
2. whose car had broken down
3. didn't want him to be year representative
4. waves to his fans and sings with the music
5. he says he is Bob
6. study the same subject as his brother
7. Nicola Sturgis

Task B

1 true, 2 false, 3 true, 4 true, 5 true, 6 false, 7 true

Task C

BRITSTYLE FILMS
LIFE AND STYLE VIDEOS AND FILMS

1. Name: _Dave_ Williams.
   Address: 4, Old London Road
   Manford   CF2 3RT

2. Favourite British or American film star: **Bruce Lee**

3. Favourite type of film: **action films**

4. Why favourite film? **fighting, loud music**

5. How often do you go to the cinema? **4 times a year**

6. Who do you go with? **a good friend**

2003-5

> **Realschulabschluss Englisch in Mecklenburg-Vorpommern**
> **Abschlussprüfung 2003: Reading Comprehension**

Top Teen Twins

The next time you hear someone say that teens are lazy, tell them about Mary-Kate and Ashley Olsen. These US twins are actresses, producers, authors, publishers and business-women – all at the same time. Last year the two 15-year-olds were so successful that they made $ 500 million!
5 You know Mary-Kate and Ashley from the hit RTL2 TV series *Full House*, where they took turns playing one character, Michelle Tanner. Since making that series, they have built their own media empire. And US kids love them. Every day the twins get hundreds of e-mails from their fans.
Mary-Kate and Ashley have their own lifestyle magazine for girls, called *mary-
10 kateandashley*. But that's not all. They also have their own fashion line with clothing, jewellery and accessories. On their website you can check out and buy all their stuff. But you can also get entertainment tips, your horoscope and inspiring information for the "mind, body and soul". Now that's cool.
But how did the Californian twins get started? When they were making *Full House*, Mary-
15 Kate and Ashley were small children. But TV polls in the USA said they were as popular as the famous TV comedian Bill Cosby! So at the age of six they formed a production company with their manager, Robert Thorne. They started making CDs and videos. That made them the world's youngest producers. Then the girls started making movies and appearing on US soap operas. In 1998 they were given their own TV series called *Two of
20 A Kind*. Last year they started their magazine, and got another TV series, called *So Little Time*.
But what are these girls like when they're not working? Mary-Kate and Ashley live with their mom Jarnie, their younger sister Lizzie and their older brother Trent in Los Angeles. Their mom and dad Dave got divorced when the twins were nine but they see their father a
25 lot. They say they lead normal teenage lives. During the day, they attend a private school in Los Angeles, where they are very well behaved. The girl's hobbies are shopping (and arguing about clothes!), going to the movies, 'N Sync, cheerleading and Tae Bo. Mary-Kate loves riding her two horses, CD and Star. Ashley enjoys dancing and tennis. Amazingly, the girls only get $ 10 a week pocket money. Friends of the twins say that they
30 think alike, but Mary-Kate, who is two minutes older, says she and Ashley are "totally different".
The Olsens say they are positive role models for young American girls: the twins are pretty, blonde and healthy-looking, they dress smartly but not sexily, and they have
35 not a single body piercing. They have not even had their ears pierced. They are the most successful child stars in America, but they haven't let it go to their heads, and above all they don't just want to have fun. "We're able to help kids and lead them on the right track," Mary-Kate told one inter-
40 viewer.
The secret of the girls' success is their niceness and their attitude towards a clean life: "No sex, no drugs, no rock 'n' roll," the girls say. Sounds like a clean way to a lot of money!

adapted from Spot on 05/2002, www.spoton.de

Aufgaben

I. Comprehension

1. Matching exercise. Combine the matching parts of the sentences: (6 p.)

   (1) The two girls prove that
   (2) The twins' success does not only come from filming, but
   (3) Their popularity began
   (4) They have become role models for US girls also because of
   (5) Despite their success
   (6) Their success is based

   a) with a TV series.
   b) Mary-Kate and Ashley don't show off.
   c) on their idea of a clean way of living.
   d) from other media and fashion businesses as well.
   e) not all teenagers are lazy nowadays.
   f) the way they look and their helpfulness.

   Put the correct letters below the numbers.

(1)	(2)	(3)	(4)	(5)	(6)

2. Read the text carefully. Find out which statements are true and which are false. Mark with a cross. true false (8 p.)

   a) Mary-Kate and Ashley played the same character in a famous TV series. ☐☐
   b) They have not become very famous in their home country yet. ☐☐
   c) A US survey compared their popularity to that of Bill Cosby. ☐☐
   d) They have even had their own TV series. ☐☐
   e) They live with their parents. ☐☐
   f) Mary-Kate's hobby is buying CDs. ☐☐
   g) Mary-Kate thinks that her way of thinking is different from her sister's. ☐☐
   h) They are against taking drugs. ☐☐

II. Language

1. Completion (11 p.)

   Almost everybody knows and watches them – soap operas. But do you know anything about the historical background of soap operas? The following information was on the Internet, but wasn't printed out properly. Reconstruct the text and find out.
   Pay attention: There are more words than gaps
   abuse – time – for – popular – see – of – early – happiness – over – unthinkable – who – such – how – discussion – watch – by – loneliness

   The soap opera began in the (1) _____ 1930s in America with 15 minute romantic daytime radio episodes about people with whom

2003-7

listeners, mostly women at home, identified. Because these series were extremely (2) _____ they were sponsored by big manufacturers of soaps and detergents, such as Procter and Gamble, Lever Brothers and Colgate Palmolive. At that (3) _____ the word 'soap opera' was created: "soap" stood for the products that were advertised and "opera" stood for the exaggerated stories.
By the mid-1950s soap operas were then 30 minutes long. People could (4) _____ them in the late morning and early afternoon every weekday.
And when you think (5) _____ the time between the 1930s and the 1950s, the classical American soap opera was typically a series about a middle-class family living in a small town.
By the 1970s, the style and content of soap operas had undergone a revolution. There was an open (6) _____ of such matters as abortion, sexually transmitted diseases and drug (7) _____.
Since the 1980s, series (8) _____ as "Dallas" and "Dynasty" have become famous all over the world. They are sagas about the super-rich with their glamorous lifestyles, who are looking (9) _____ real love. But again and again the soaps show that even rich people have problems and that money does not buy (10) _____. In fact that's one of the reasons the viewers like them so much.
Indeed, today TV programmes without soaps are (11) _____.

2. Using the dictionary (3 p.)

The following words from the text have various meanings. Which of the meanings given in the dictionary is the one used in the text? Underline the best German translation.

Text: *You know Mary-Kate and Ashley from ... Full House, where they took turns playing one character, Michelle Tanner.*

take turns (line 6)

| **take** I s *(Film, TV):* Einstellung II v/tr *(irr)* **1.** nehmen **2.** mitnehmen **3.** *(Verantwortung)* auf sich nehmen **4.** bringen **5.** *(Film, Foto)* machen | **6.** ~ **away** wegnehmen **7.** ~ **a note of s.th.** etw. notieren **8.** ~ **turns** sich abwechseln II v/tr ~ **after sb.** jemandem ähneln |

Text: *But you can also get entertainment tips, your horoscope and inspiring information for the "mind, body and soul".*

mind (line 13)

| **mind** I s **1.** Ansicht, Meinung **to my** ~ meiner Ansicht nach **2.** Verstand, Geist **3.** Neigung, Lust | II v/tr **1.** achtgeben auf **2.** aufpassen, sehen nach III v/itr etwas dagegen haben |

Text: *"We're able to help kids and lead them on the right track," ...*

track (line 39)

| **track** I s **1.** Fährte **2.** Weg, Pfad **3.** *(Renn-, Aschen)* Bahn II v/tr **1.** *(jdn. eine Spur)* verfolgen | **2.** aufspüren III v/itr **1.** *mot* Spur halten **2.** *film* sich bewegen **3.** Fährten lesen |

3. Using words of the same family. Complete each sentence with the suitable word given below the sentence. (4 p.)

a) Many parents are worried that it is not _____ for their children to be out on the streets, so the youngsters are given computers and TVs.
(safety – save – safe)

b) The Internet's _____ has increased over the years.
(popularity – popularize – popular)

c) Children _____ computers more often at home than at school.
(usage – use – useful)

d) There are _____ between girls and boys in the usage of PCs.
(differences – differ – different)

III. Using structures/Passing on messages

1. Hakan Tuncer from Turkey wants to describe a modern day addiction to computers. In some places he isn't sure what to write. How would you decide? Underline your suggestion. (13 p.)

Right now, a "new generation" addiction _____¹ quickly all over the world. Webaholism affects people of different ages. They _____² the net, use e-mail, and speak in chat rooms. They spend many hours at the computer, and it becomes something like an addiction. They cannot stop, and it influences their _____³. Ten years ago, no one _____⁴ that using computers could become a behaviour that could change the lives of computer users. For many years this addiction _____⁵ teenagers and college students.

They become hooked on computers and slowly their school life and friendship _____⁶ by this situation. They spend all their free time surfing and _____⁷ on their homework, so this addiction influences their grades and success at school. They spend more time in front of computers than with friends. Their relationships with their friends _____⁸. Their virtual life becomes _____⁹ than their real life. They have a new language that they speak in the chat rooms and it causes cultural changes in normal life. Because of the change in their behaviour, they begin to isolate themselves from society and live with their virtual friends. They share their emotions and feelings with "friends" _____¹⁰ they have never met. Although they feel _____¹¹ confident on the computer, they are not confident with real friends they have known for a long time.

If they _____¹² online all night long, they won't get enough sleep. Finally they can say that they are addicted to chatrooms. This _____¹³ a serious problem for our society in the future.

adapted from: Topics_mag@yahoo.com

1	A	is spreading	B	spreads	C	spread
2	A	surf	B	are surfing	C	surfed
3	A	life	B	lives	C	live
4	A	have thought	B	thought	C	has thought

5	A	influenced	B	influences	C	has influenced
6	A	will manipulate	B	is manipulated	C	manipulates
7	A	don't concentrate	B	concentrate not	C	didn't concentrate
8	A	changes	B	changing	C	change
9	A	most important	B	more important	C	important
10	A	which	B	what	C	who
11	A	perfectly	B	perfect	C	more perfectly
12	A	stayed	B	would stay	C	stay
13	A	will be	B	is	C	was

2. You've got some short messages from Mary-Kate and Ashley for the sales manager. Explain to him in German what they mean. (3 p.)

   new fashion line to come in July

   3 mio CDs produced in 2002

   unable to attend party

3. There is a German visitor in the *mary-kateandashley* office building. Tell her what the following signs mean. (3 p.)

   Ring 008811 to place an advertisement in this paper

   NO PARKING ENTRANCE USED 24 HOURS A DAY

   Security cameras in use around this building

2003-10

IV. Using the language in different contexts (6 p.)

1. Information gap task. You have a lot more questions than the text *Top Teen Twins* could answer.
   What else would you like to know? Ask Mary-Kate and Ashley 3 different kinds of questions that haven't been answered yet.

   a) _____

   b) _____

   c) _____

2. Questionnaire (18 p.)

   An American magazine wants to find out about some aspects of European teenagers' lives.

   Please fill in the questionnaire in the magazine. Answer all the questions. Please give reasons for your answers. Write at least 80 words altogether. Count your words.

   a) What's your idea of a good job?

   b) Name a few things you could do without in your life.

   c) What do you think of piercing?

   d) What would you call a positive role model?

   e) What's your opinion on soap operas?

   f) What would happen if your mobile phone beeped in the lesson?

V. Comment/Giving opinion

Write down your opinion on **one** of the following statements.
Give reasons for your opinion using examples where possible.
Write about 150 words altogether. Count your words. (25 p.)

- Mobile phones are a fashion that is useful but not really necessary.
- Money can't buy friendship.
- Personality is more important than looks.
- Teenagers these days have too much freedom.
- The media have a strong influence especially on teenagers.
- Young people can't imagine living without e-mail or chat-rooms.
- Being out of work can make people ill.
- Every teenager dreams of being a millionaire.
- Sport is only big money.

Lösung

I. Comprehension

1.

(1)	(2)	(3)	(4)	(5)	(6)
e	d	a	f	b	c

2. a) true   b) false
   c) true   d) true
   e) false   f) false
   g) true   h) true

II. Language

1. (1) early, (2) popular, (3) time, (4) watch, (5) of, (6) discussion, (7) abuse, (8) such, (9) for, (10) happiness, (11) unthinkable

2. take: II 8   sich abwechseln
   mind: I 2   Verstand, Geist
   track: I 2   Weg, Pfad

3. a) safe   b) popularity
   c) use   d) differences

III. Using structures

1. Webaholism
   1. A <u>is spreading</u>   (Hinweis: Signalwort = now, Present Progressive)
   2. A <u>surf</u>   (Hinweis: allgemeingültige Aussage, Simple Present)

2003-12

3. **B** lives (Hinweis: Signalwort = their, Mehrzahl)
4. **B** thought (Hinweis: Signalwort = years ago, Simple Past)
5. **C** has influenced (Hinweis: Signalwort = for many years, Simple Present Perfect)
6. **B** is manipulated (Hinweis: Signalwort = by, Passiv, Simple Present)
7. **A** don't concentrate (Hinweis : Signalwort = they, 3. Person, Mehrzahl)
8. **C** change (Hinweis: Signalwort = relationships, Mehrzahl)
9. **B** more important (Hinweis: Signalwort = than, Vergleich/Komparativ des Adjektives)
10. **C** who (Hinweis: Signalwort = friends, Personen)
11. **A** perfectly (Hinweis: das Adjektiv **confident** wird näher bestimmt = Adverb)
12. **C** stay (Hinweis: Hauptsatz = Simple Future, if-Satz = Simple Present)
13. **A** will be (Hinweis: Signalwort = in the future, Simple Future)

2. Short messages
   – Die neue Modelinie wird im Juli (heraus)kommen.
   – Im Jahre 2002 wurden 3 Millionen CDs produziert.
   – Mary-Kate und Ashley können nicht an der Party teilnehmen.

3. Public notices/signs
   – Um eine Anzeige in dieser Zeitung zu schalten, müssen Sie 008811 anrufen.
   – Hier ist Parkverbot, weil der Eingang 24 Stunden lang genutzt wird.
   – Im Gebäude/ums Gebäude herum befinden sich Sicherheitskameras.

IV. Using the language in different contexts

1. a) Do you have a boy-friend?
   b) What are your role models?
   c) How do you get along with your brother and your younger sister?

2. a) Well, my idea of a good job is working with computers because I am very good at operating them.
   b) I could live without clothes with brand names because many people I know attach too much importance to them and their judgement is often influenced by these superficial things.
   I could also do without drugs because I think they are dangerous and not necessary for life to be exciting.
   c) Many of my friends say that piercings are a must today but I do not like piercings and I do not think it is healthy.
   d) I would call a positive role model a person who leads an active and clean life because being active and clean makes people happy with themselves and confident.
   e) I would say prime time TV would be unthinkable without soap operas. That is the reason why I also have a favourite soap that offers me a world different from my own, but I am not hooked on this daily programme and I do realize that soap operas do not show real life.
   f) Mobile phones are not allowed at my school, so I have to leave it at home.

V. Comment/Giving opinion

Hinweis: In dieser Aufgabe sollst du dich mit einem von dir gewählten Statement (Behauptung, Feststellung) auseinandersetzen. Formuliere deine Meinung, begründe diese und versuche, Beispiele u. a. aus deinem Erfahrungsbereich heranzuziehen. Achte darauf, deine schriftlichen Äußerungen logisch zu gliedern und auf die bereits bekannten Wendungen zurückzugreifen.

- **Mobile phones are a fashion that is useful but not really necessary**
  The development of new technologies has made our life more convenient, safer and easier. In my opinion the mobile phone is one of the greatest inventions of our time. That is the reason why I have chosen the statement, although I cannot agree with it.
  It is true that mobile phones are a fashion, but above all they are not only useful but very important gadgets. With a mobile phone you can call anybody, anywhere, any time. Information can be transmitted very fast and the service offered by mobile phones has made our lives more convenient.
  My parents bought me a mobile to be able to keep in touch with me. They also feel safe because they know that in emergencies or serious situations I could call for help. So my parents also think that mobiles are very necessary because they do not only give users a feeling of security.
  Furthermore, I think mobile phones save a lot of time because there are a lot of services you can use.
  To sum up, I would say that a mobile is an important, timesaving, useful, convenient and necessary device.

- **Money can't buy friendship**
  It is true that it is becoming more and more difficult to make real friends, but I am still convinced that money can't buy friendship, so I fully agree with this statement.
  We meet a lot of people every day but do we call them all friends? I have chosen my friends very carefully. I do not attach great importance to a person's appearance, clothes or belongings.
  Character traits and manners are more important to me. To my mind, honesty and sincerity are a basis for a real friendship. Furthermore, I think a friend must be critical of my faults, because a friendship should make a contribution to the development of my personality.
  Common interests and hobbies are also important for a friendship. However, it takes time to find out whether a person can be a real friend or not.
  I know some people who do not realize what friendship means. They are generous, and try to impress others with their money, but do they find real friends? I think most of their "friends" only take advantage of them. I can only feel sorry for them.
  I have come to the conclusion that nowadays it seems to be more difficult to make real friends but I believe that a good friendship improves the quality of life and it does not cost any money.

- **Personality is more important than looks**
  It is a sad fact that more and more people attach great importance to appearance and clothes. But "it is not only fine feathers that make fine birds". I think this statement is absolutely true.
  People are often influenced in their judgement by such superficial things as a person's appearance, but I am sure that most people looking for a partner prefer such attributes as honesty, sincerity and reliability.

Almost all of my friends dream of getting married and having children. We have certain ideas about our future partners, but looks and appearance are not important. Character traits and manners are more convincing than looks or clothes. Confidence serves as a basis for a good partnership, but somebody's beautiful eyes do not show whether the person is trustworthy or not.
That is the reason why I am convinced that personality is not only more important than looks but is fundamental to starting a partnership.

- **Teenagers these days have too much freedom**
You often hear adults say that being a teenager is the best time of your life with much freedom and without any worries. And there are also many people who think that we teenagers have too much freedom nowadays.
I do not doubt that we teenagers enjoy our lives but we do not have too much freedom. So it will not be surprising that I can only partly agree with this statement.
To my mind, freedom means independence. But can a teenager really be independent? Most teenagers live at home, go to school or college, or work as apprentices. That means we depend on our parents.
Well, my mother and father give me love and security, but they are also very strict and set me limits. They forbid me to stay out longer than midnight at weekends, for instance. They always keep an eye on me. But I also know from friends that there are parents who do not set their children limits. It is not surprising that teenagers make the most of this. But in my opinion this freedom is only carelessness which is risky and dangerous.
To sum up, I would stress that it depends on the parents whether teenagers have too much freedom or not.

- **The media have a strong influence especially on teenagers**
Life without the media is unthinkable today. That is the reason why the media have a stronger influence on our lives than we want to admit.
Teenagers especially are easily influenced because they do not have much experience of life.
Therefore, I am afraid I have to agree with the statement.
Teenagers are not often critical of the media and their large variety of entertainment, services and information. But I think that it depends on the individual whether this influence is positive or negative.
Watching TV or surfing the Internet, for example, can be very useful. There are a lot of TV programmes with a high standard of education to broaden viewers' knowledge. And the Internet is an enormous databank and unlimited source of information. However, there are also negative influences. More and more you can see people, and especially teenagers, sitting in front of the TV set or the computer instead of spending time with their family and friends. There are too many violent programmes and computer games available. Several incidents have shown that violence on the screen can cause aggression in real life.
To sum up, I would say the last word is always with the people. The media have opened up a new world for us which must be handled with care and responsibility.

- **Young people can't imagine living without e-mail and chat-rooms**
Surfing the Internet, sending e-mails and "meeting" people in chat-rooms are my favourite spare time activities, which is why I have chosen this statement. I can fully agree with it. In my opinion the Internet is one of the greatest inventions of our time. Moreover, the Internet is the best place to meet different people. Since I have been using the net and its services I have already chatted to people of all ages and many nationalities. It is very interesting and exciting to get to know people in chat-rooms. It will be not surprising that my friends agree with me. We are also enthusiastic about

the opportunity of sending e-mails by mobile phones, because you do not need to be at home in front of the computer to send and receive "important" information via the Internet. Finally, I want to emphasize that it is not an exaggeration to say that we young people cannot do without e-mail and chat-rooms.

- **Being out of work can make people ill**
Unfortunately I have to agree with this statement. Being out of work is a problem which faces a lot of people in our country. In our region especially there is a high unemployment rate. As my father has been unemployed for more than 13 months I can judge such a situation. For my father being out of work means that he is useless. He is very disappointed and dissatisfied with the situation. It is not only the fact of not earning any money but of having no motivation. My father has become unhappy and depressed. He refuses the help of our family and friends. For some weeks he has only left our house to go to the employment office. I am very sad because I have to watch my father suffering from unemployment.
For several weeks he has had stomach trouble and he has been worse from day to day. But my mother and I do not give up encouraging him. To sum up, I have to say that it is a sad truth that being out of work can make people ill.

- **Every teenager dreams of being a millionaire**
Well, I do not know a single person who does not want to have a lot of money. So I would say the statement does not only go for teenagers. Not having any financial worries and the opportunity to be able to afford almost anything is a very attractive idea. In fact, money is very necessary in people's lives because consumption plays an important role in our society. "Money buys happiness" is a common opinion. Is there anybody who does not want to be happy?
Teenagers especially want to lead independent and exciting lives. Enough money makes new experiences and travelling to other countries possible. These things are also more pleasant than being afraid of not finding a job. To my mind, one reason why almost everyone dreams of being a millionaire is the growing social uncertainty. The high rate of unemployment causes anxiety.
To sum up, I would say that everyone, not only teenagers, wants to live without financial worries and problems.

- **Sport is only big money**
Sport is often business and this means sport is money, so I can agree with the above-mentioned statement. But I would say that there are special kinds of sports which have been big money for several years. Tennis, soccer or basketball, for example, are sports where sportsmen and women, managers and a lot of other people earn (too) much money. To my mind, sport has become entertainment and therefore a product of a certain type of industry. This industry would be unthinkable without advertising and sponsoring. But this industry can only be successful because there are enough fans of such entertainment. However, I do not want question the performance of the tennis or soccer or basketball players. They are very professional and they also often put their health at risk.
Finally, I want to stress that some kinds of sports are big money and are very popular with millions of people.

> **Realschulabschluss Englisch in Mecklenburg-Vorpommern**
> **Abschlussprüfung 2004: Hörverstehen**

You're surely interested in music and stars. First you're going to listen to a fan's phone call at a box office and after that you'll learn more about two of his stars. Their names are famous: Robbie Williams and Kelly Osbourne.

Task A: Musical Booking Form

Good morning, I'd like to go to the musical *Rock me to Heaven* at the Adelphi. Could you tell me which tickets are still available?
The date? Oh yes, for Saturday, 24th July.
Only two prices available, £ 35 and £ 50! That's very expensive. Well, I suppose I'd better
5 take the tickets for £ 50 'cos it's my girlfriend's birthday. Could I have two tickets, please?
Could I pay by credit card? Yes, that's good.
You'd like the details. It's a Mastercard and the number is 6190 0606 5432 7831.
Yes, I'll repeat that: 6190 0606 5432 7831. It's valid till June 2006, that's 06/06
Could you please send me the tickets? I'll give you my address. It's 47 Market Square,
10 Westbury, Wiltshire. I'll spell Westbury, W-e-s-t-b-u-r-y. The postcode is BA13 3DZ.
Yes, that's right BA13 3DZ.
Oh, I forgot my name, it's Alex Smithers. Is that all? OK. Thanks, bye.

Task B: Robbie Williams

The famous British pop singer Robbie Williams celebrated his 30th birthday last February.
He first started singing when he was only three years old.
His mother Janet says, "We went on holiday to Spain and there was a talent show for children. Robbie went on stage and sang *Summer Nights* from the musical called *Grease*.
5 Everybody loved him."
Janet wanted Robbie to go to university. But he had other plans. He left school at the age of 16 and joined a band. *Take That* became the biggest British band since the *Beatles*. They sold millions of CDs. But Robbie got tired of being in a boy band. He wanted to make his own music.
10 Robbie left *Take That* in 1995 to go solo. He had a bad start. He drank too much, took too many drugs and went into hospital for rehabilitation. His first CD, *Life Thru a Lens,* only sold 30,000 copies in its first six months. But later, in July 1997, Robbie produced the song *Angels*. It was a huge hit and he became a big star. Today Robie has sold more than 20 million CDs. Last year he signed the second-biggest record deal in history. It earned
15 him £ 80 million.
Robbie is famous for provoking people. But sometimes he goes too far. In August 2000, he produced a video for *Rock DJ*. In the video, he pulls his skin and muscles from his body. He says, "I wanted to make a video that would make people sick. It was a big joke."
Not everybody thought such a kind of "joke" was funny. Some countries banned the video.
20 Others only showed part of it.
But the video didn't stop people buying Robbie's music. His concerts have been sold out for months.

adapted from Spot on 07/2003: Talitha Linehan Singing and Winning

Task C: Kelly Osbourne on what made 2003 so special for her

Hi! My name's Kelly Osbourne and I think I've always been different. When I was still a baby my father Ozzy Osbourne took me with him around the world in a tour bus. You see, he was a famous rock star and wanted to have his family around when he gave concerts. When I was 13 my family moved from England to the US. This was when I started
5 wearing crazy clothes. I also began collecting chairs. That was great fun.
I hated school. I had terrible teachers who always told me what to do. I didn't like that and I really didn't learn very much. And in *my* school in America the other kids made fun of me because of my British accent. I hated it all and so I left school when I was 15. Of course my parents didn't like that at all. But what could they do?
10 I started singing and writing my own songs. Writing songs is easy. I was surprised. My first song, a cover version of a *Madonna* song, was a huge hit and now I'm proud to be on tour with Robbie Williams. This is something that made 2003 special for me. And there's another thing. It's my family. You know we are a happy, crazy family. That's why MTV has been filming me and my family at home. Do you know *The Osbournes?* That's us!
15 Today millions of people watch our reality series and love it. It has made me a star. I don't mind having TV cameras in our home. But to be honest, I'd never watch our show myself. That's like sitting on the loo and watching yourself in the mirror. I think this is embarrassing.

adapted from Spot on 8/2003 and J17 July 2003

Aufgaben

Task A: Musical Booking Form

There is a musical on and this young person phones to book some tickets.
Listen to what he says and fill in the missing information. (6 p.)

Musical Booking Form

NAME OF MUSICAL _____ *Rock me to Heaven* _____

LOCATION _____ *Adelphi* _____

DAY & DATE OF CONCERT *Saturday,* _____ (0,5 p)

TICKET PRICES AVAILABLE _____ (1 p)

NUMBER OF TICKETS BOOKED _____ (0,5 p)

PRICE PER TICKET BOOKED _____ (0,5 p)

CUSTOMER'S NAME _____ *Smithers* _____ (0,5 p)

CUSTOMER'S ADDRESS _____ (1 p)

_____ , *Wiltshire* _____ (0,5 p)

POSTCODE _____ (0,5 p)

CREDIT CARD DETAILS Number _____ (1 p)

Expiry Date _____ *06/06* _____

Task B: Robbie Williams

Listen to the report and tick the correct information. There is only one answer per item. (7 p.)

1. At the age of three Robbie sang
   - [ ] a song from a musical.
   - [ ] about summer love in Greece.
   - [ ] a song about holidays in Spain.

2. When Robbie was 16 years old he
   - [ ] wanted to go to university.
   - [ ] smoked a joint.
   - [ ] became a member of a band.

3. Robbie left *Take That* because
   - [ ] he wanted to produce music of his own.
   - [ ] he was tired.
   - [ ] he didn't like boy bands.

4. When he started as a solo singer Robbie
   - [ ] was involved in drugs.
   - [ ] didn't go into rehabilitation.
   - [ ] sold only 3,000 copies of his first CD.

5. Robbie's video for *Rock* DJ was produced because
   - [ ] he was sick.
   - [ ] it was big fun.
   - [ ] he wanted to make people sick.

6. The video was
   - [ ] banned by several countries.
   - [ ] shown everywhere.
   - [ ] funny for everybody.

7. Robbie's concerts
   - [ ] stopped people buying his video.
   - [ ] were sold out in spite of his video.
   - [ ] were stopped for months.

Task C: Kelly Osbourne on what made 2003 so special for her

Try to find out if the following information is true or false. (7 p.)

	true	false
1. Kelly travelled around the world when she was very young.	☐	☐
2. Kelly's father didn't like to be on tour without his family.	☐	☐
3. As a teenager Kelly still used to dress like everybody else.	☐	☐
4. Kelly left school only because she was bullied by other kids.	☐	☐
5. The first song that Kelly wrote was for Madonna.	☐	☐
6. Kelly is positive about her family.	☐	☐
7. Kelly enjoys sitting and watching *The Osbournes* on TV.	☐	☐

Lösung

Task A

Musical Booking Form

NAME OF MUSICAL   Rock me to Heaven
LOCATION   Adelphi
DAY & DATE OF CONCERT   Saturday, 24th July
TICKET PRICES AVAILABLE 35 and 50 Pounds
NUMBER OF TICKETS BOOKED two
PRICE PER TICKET BOOKED 50 Pounds
CUSTOMER'S NAME   Alex Smithers
CUSTOMER'S ADDRESS   47 Market Square
                         Westbury, Wiltshire
POSTCODE   BA 13 3 DZ
CREDIT CARD DETAILS Number 6190 0606 5432 7831
                     Expiry Date 06/06

Task B
1. a song from a musical
2. became a member of a band
3. he wanted to produce music of his own
4. was involved in drugs
5. he wanted to make people sick
6. banned by several countries
7. were sold out in spite of his video

Task C
1. true, 2. true, 3. false, 4. false, 5. false, 6. true, 7. false

> Realschulabschluss Englisch in Mecklenburg-Vorpommern
> Abschlussprüfung 2004: Reading Comprehension

Eminem

His real name is Marshall Bruce Mathers III. He is pop music's most controversial, and many say, best rapper. On the one hand, he has his critics, who say he is a dangerous influence on children because of his hateful, racist, dirty lyrics. On the other hand, he is loved by teenagers and had a great success with his last album, *The Marshall Mathers LP,*
5 which sold five million copies in the first month in the US alone.

His latest album, *The Eminem Show,* is also enjoying much success. But is he really the bad boy he makes himself out to be, or is he just trying to shock us and is really quite a sweetie?

He was born in Kansas City, Missouri on October 17, 1974. He never met his father, and
10 was brought up by his mother, Debbie Mathers. They moved around a lot until they settled in Detroit. He was a shy child. Not good at school, he preferred to read comic books and listen to rap music. After school he had various dead-end jobs, while he tried to create a rap style of his own.

With fame and success in the rap world, his personal life became even more unstable.
15 His mum filed a law suit against him in 1999, because of the insulting comments he had made about her in his songs and in interviews. Their relationship does not seem to have improved.

On his latest album, *The Eminem Show,* in the song *Cleaning out the Closet,* Eminem raps:

> *Ma, remember when Ronnie died and you said you wished it was me?/ Well, guess*
> 20 *what, I'm as dead to you as can be.*

His love life has also been unstable. He married Kim in 1999. Kim had lived with Eminem and his mum since she was 12 and at first they had a brother – sister relationship. They divorced in 2001. They have a child called Hailie who is six. He also raps about Kim on his latest album with much hatred. His most recent tattoo suggests she should "rot in
25 pieces".

So what is the secret of his success? Some say he is an anti-hero, speaking for outcast youth. He is against conservative, conformist, patriotic America and the opposite of the goody-two-
30 shoes[1] pop stars such as Britney Spears or the Backstreet Boys. He raps for millions of teenagers who feel out of place and not listened to in adult society.

At the top of the charts, he is also a critic of
35 fame. In *Without Me,* from the new album, he raps:

> *Not the first king of controversy/*
> *I am the worst thing since Elvis Presley/*
> *To do black music so selfishly/*
> 40 *And use it to make myself wealthy.*

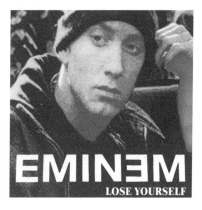

2004-5

His mum said his music managers turned a sweet, shy, sensitive boy into a shock-rapper. But Eminem himself tries to show a nicer side in *Hailie's Song*, a song about his daughter on the latest album: *People make jokes, they don't see my real side.*

So what is Eminem really like? Can we believe there is a nice side to someone who raps so many not-nice things?

adapted from READ ON, November Issue 2002

1 lammfromm

Aufgaben

I. Comprehension

1. Matching exercise. Combine the matching parts of the sentences: (6 p.)

   (1) The text tries to
   (2) Eminem is criticised
   (3) Teenagers love him
   (4) Growing popularity has caused
   (5) Eminem represents millions of youngsters who
   (6) Eminem's mother says he has changed in personality

   a) a lot of instability in his private life.
   b) because of his managers.
   c) analyse what's real about Eminem's image.
   d) feel rejected by society.
   e) for being bad for kids.
   f) although his lyrics are nasty.

   Put the correct letters below the numbers.

(1)	(2)	(3)	(4)	(5)	(6)

2. True or false?
   Read the text carefully. Find out which statements are true and which are false. Mark with a cross. (8 p.)

true	false	
		a) The texts of some of Eminem's songs are racist.
		b) He has seen his father face to face.
		c) He did not have a permanent job after leaving school.
		d) Eminem praised his mother in a rap text.
		e) Kim is Eminem's sister.
		f) Eminem has got a daughter.
		g) He respects conservative people in his home country.
		h) Eminem knows that people don't recognise the positive aspects in his personality.

II. Language

1. Completion (11 p.)

... *Why do they laugh at me? Other people can be very rude* ... These words are part of what Sandy, a 16-year-old girl from Coventry, wrote to a teenage magazine. You'll find the answer for Sandy when you use the words below to reconstruct the text.
Be careful, there are more words than gaps.
will – crime – with – how – belong – feel – lot – about – friendly – hair – hurts – as – offensive – want – works – like

---

Sandy Pearson
20 Ivybride Road
Coventry CV3 5PH

Problems & Letters
J17, Endeavour House
189 Shaftsbury Avenue
London WC2H 8J

Dear Sandy,

You _____¹ to a group of rockers in your hometown. You wear baggy jeans, all sorts of chains, coloured jumpers and a _____² of piercings. People who pass you on the streets say _____³ things about you and your clothes. Everybody can imagine how much this _____⁴. But you keep dressing differently because you don't want to look _____⁵ normal people. You spend time with your friends and this is the best time of your life. It's a time when you believe that you are different and very special. Of course you use your clothes to _____⁶ good. As a group of special people you have learned to cope _____⁷ difficult situations. At your age you _____⁸ to change things. This is the privilege of youth and I hope you'll try hard to do so. The world needs you. There are many ways to express your ideas and attitude towards life. Other teens get their _____⁹ dyed bright colours or have tattoos on their bodies just to look good. You can dress just _____¹⁰ you like. What you are inside is more important than what you seem to be. Don't worry _____¹¹ what people think.

Do your own thing,

J17

2. Using the dictionary (3 p.)

The following words from the text have various meanings. Which of the meanings given in the dictionary is the one used in the text? Underline the best German translation.

Text: *But is he really the bad boy he makes himself out to be, ...*

make out (line 7)
make out I v/tr 1.ausfindig machen, herausbekommen, entziffern 2. *(Liste)* aufstellen 3. *(Formular)* ausfüllen
4. *(Rechnung, Scheck)* ausstellen 5. behaupten **II** v/itr 1. weiter-, vorwärtskommen *fig* Erfolg haben 2. auskommen, zurechtkommen *(with mit)*

Text: *He never met his father and was brought up by his mother, Debbie Mathers.*

bring (line 10)
bring (brought) v 1. (mit-, her)bringen 2. *jdn* dazu bringen **(to do** zu tun) 3. **~ about** zustande bringen, bewirken
4. **~ up** auf-, großziehen, erziehen 5. **~ up** zur Sprache bringen 6. **- up** *bsd. Brt. etw.* (er)brechen

Text: *His mum said his music managers turned a sweet, shy, sensitive boy into a shockrapper.*

turn (line 41)
turn I s 1. Drehung 2. *(Straße)* Kurve, *Sport* Wende 3. Reihenfolge 4. (guter) Dienst 5. *med* Anfall 6. Tendenz, Hang, Neigung **II** v/tr 1. drehen, antreiben 2. *(Kopf)* drehen, wenden 3. *(Heu, Kragen, Auto)* wenden, *(Seite)* umblättern 4. *(Gedanken, Blicke)* richten **III** v/itr 1. sich drehen, sich drehen lassen 2. *(Fahrer, Auto)* abbiegen,
wenden 3. *(Blätter)* sich färben; *(Wetter)* umschlagen **IV** *(mit Präposition)* **turn about** v/itr umdrehen, kehrtmachen; **turn away** v/tr fort-, wegschicken; **turn in** v/itr 1. *(Auto)* einbiegen 2. *fam* zu Bett gehen; **turn into** v/itr sich verwandeln in, v/tr verwandeln in; **turn on** v/tr 1. aufdrehen 2. einschalten 3. anmachen

3. Using words of the same family. Complete each sentence with the suitable word given below the sentence. (4 p.)

   a) Many young people _____ strongly with their pop idols.
      (identity – identify – identical)

   b) Singers like Marilyn Manson make an enormous _____ on some youngsters.
      (impression – impress – impressive)

   c) Some of the most creative musicians have been _____ on alcohol and drugs.
      (dependence – depend – dependent)

   d) Always remember: turn down the music to _____ your hearing.
      (protection – protect – protective)

III. Using structures / Passing on messages

1. Per Amundson from Sweden wants to describe a recent phenomenon in the Swedish music scene for a British pop magazine. In some places he isn't sure what to write. How would you decide? Underline your suggestion. (10 p.)

Have your parents told you that they love you? And that you can ask them any question you want? Well, here's one. In a quiet moment, ask your mother whether she _____¹ ever danced to *Super Trouper*. Or was she ever the *Dancing Queen* when she was young? *Mamma Mia*, that _____² 25 years ago! And your father – does he only think of history when he hears the word *Waterloo*?

Probably not. All of these were top-ten hits when your parents were teenagers. And this millennium brought these hit songs back again! Even the music business _____³ about the *A*Teens* and their versions of old *ABBA* songs. Never before in the history of pop music has a band copied original songs so _____⁴ (and made so much money out of it!).

Almost 30 years ago, a group of four Swedes started a music group. The first letters of their names became the group's name: *ABBA*. Every record they made was a huge hit. All over the world people knew the name *ABBA*. Can history repeat _____⁵? It seems it can. Now there are the *A*Teens*. They're also from Sweden and they _____⁶ good friends for three years. In a recent TV interview one of them revealed that a record company chose them out of 30 boys and girls at a dance school and called them *ABBA TEENS*. Later, the name _____⁷ to *A*Teens*.

"We like the *ABBA* lyrics", the *A*Teens* confess. However, many people think the lyrics are very silly. But _____⁸ really cares. *ABBA* songs are happy, catchy and fun. The *A*Teens* have never met the original *ABBA* group members _____⁹ have not recorded any new music for almost 20 years but are still very popular. The *A*Teens* continue the *ABBA* tradition. If you _____¹⁰ the electronic sound of their cover versions yet, listen to the original ABBA songs first.

adapted from: Spot on 7/2000

1	A	has	B	have	C will have
2	A	is	B	was	C has been
3	A	surprised	B	is surprised	C were surprised
4	A	successful	B	successfully	C most successful
5	A	themselves	B	herself	C itself
6	A	have been	B	are	C were
7	A	is changed	B	was changed	C has been changed
8	A	nobody	B	anybody	C somebody
9	A	which	B	who	C whose
10	A	know not	B	didn't know	C don't know

2. Your friend has got some short messages in English and isn't sure if he's understood them alright. Say what they mean in German. (3 p.)

interested in info on Jennifer Lopez? contact JLoFAN@CLUB.com

pls take next low budget flight to Edinburgh!! Miss you
Harry

remember:
film's starting earlier than advertised –
pls bring popcorn
Helen

3. The following signs were spotted at a Robbie Williams concert in London. What's their message in German? (3 p.)

**OVER 18s ONLY
Sorry no children allowed in stage area**

THIS MACHINE IS ONLY FOR THE USE OF PEOPLE AGED 16 OR OVER

Consumption of alcohol not permitted during concert

4. Neben dir und deinem Freund sitzt ein Spanier im Eminem Konzert. Da ihr die Sprache des anderen nicht sprecht, versucht ihr euch auf Englisch zu unterhalten. Dabei bittet dich dein Freund ihm bei einigen Äußerungen zu helfen: (3 p.)
(je 0,5 p. contents, 0,5 p. correctness)

a) Sage, dass Eminem besser ist als Pink.

b) Erzähle, dass du das neue Video noch nicht gesehen hast.

c) Frage, wann er zurück nach Spanien fliegt.

IV. Using the language in different contexts (3 p.)

1. Information gap task. You have a lot more questions than the text *Eminem* could answer.

   What else would you like to know? Ask Eminem, his ex-wife or his mother 3 different kinds of questions that haven't been answered yet.

   a)

   b)

   c)

2. Questionnaire (18 p.)

   An American magazine wants to find out about European teenagers' attitudes and values.

   Please fill in the questionnaire in the magazine. Answer all the questions. Please give reasons for your answers. Write at least 80 words altogether. Count your words.

   a) Do you think family life has an influence on a person's future?

   b) What makes a good music video?

c) What kind of music do you prefer?

d) What does "family" mean to you?

e) Is being wealthy part of your future plans?

f) Should music lyrics and/or videos be censored?

V. Comment/Giving opinion

Write down your opinion on **one** of the following statements.
**Give reasons for your opinion using examples where possible.
Write about 150 words altogether. Count your words.**

(25 p.)

- Role models can have both a negative and a positive effect on youngsters.
- Soaps and talk shows make you stupid.
- Teaching behaviour at school has its pros and cons.
- The values of the older generation are not ours.
- Wearing school uniforms is a good idea.
- Songs with bad language and a violent content should be censored.
- You don't have to have talent to become a superstar.

Lösung

I. Comprehension

1.

(1)	(2)	(3)	(4)	(5)	(6)
c	e	f	a	d	b

2.
   a) true
   b) false
   c) true
   d) false
   e) false
   f) true
   g) false
   h) true

II. Language

1. (1) belong, (2) lot, (3) offensive, (4) hurts, (5) like, (6) feel, (7) with, (8) want, (9) hair, (10) as, (11) about

2. make out: I 5 behaupten
   bring: 4 auf-, großziehen, erziehen
   turn: IV 2 verwandeln in

3. a) identify
   b) impression
   c) dependent
   d) protect

III. Using structures

1.
   1. **A** <u>has</u>
      (Hinweis: Signalwort = ever, Present Perfect, 3. Person Einzahl)
   2. **B** <u>was</u>
      (Hinweis: Signalwort = ago, Simple Past)
   3. **B** <u>is surprised</u>
      (Hinweis: allgemeine Aussage, Simple Present/Passiv)
   4. **B** <u>successfully</u>
      (Hinweis: Signalwort = copied = Verb = Adverb)
   5. **C** <u>itself</u>
      (Hinweis: Signalwort = history, unbelebtes Substantiv)
   6. **A** <u>have been</u>
      (Hinweis: Signalwort = for, Present Perfect)
   7. **B** <u>was changed</u>
      (Hinweis: Signalwort = later, Simple Past/Passiv)

8. **A** <u>nobody</u>
   (Hinweis: einzig sinnvolle Variante)
9. **B** <u>who</u>
   (Hinweis: Signalwort = members, Personen)
10. **C** <u>don't know</u>
    (Hinweis: Signalwort = if, Bedingungssatz, Simple Present)

2. Wenn du Interesse an Informationen über Jennifer Lopez hast, kannst du über die angegebene Adresse Kontakt mit ihrem Fan Club aufnehmen.

   Harry bittet dich den nächsten Billigflug nach Edinburgh zu nehmen, denn er vermisst dich.

   Helen erinnert dich daran, dass der Film früher als angekündigt beginnt und sie bittet dich, Popcorn mitzubringen.

3. Hier steht, dass nur Leute über 18 zugelassen sind und Kinder nicht in den Bühnenbereich dürfen.

   Man muss mindestens 16 sein, um diesen Automaten/Maschine zu benutzen.

   Das Schild weist darauf hin, dass der Konsum von Alkohol während des Konzerts verboten ist.

4. a) Eminem is better than Pink
   b) I haven't seen the new video yet.
   c) When are you going/flying back to Spain?

IV. Using the language in different contexts

1. a) Eminem, how often do you see your daughter?
   b) Debbie, why don't you try to make it up with your son?
   c) Kim, do you have contact with Eminem's mother?

2. a) Well, I think family life has a strong influence on a person's future. The love, experience and education of a parent have a particularly strong effect on a child's development.
   b) Good dancers, exciting action and a great performance by the artist make a good music video, because these things are important for good entertainment.
   c) I prefer Black music because it sounds great and there are so many remarkable musicians.
   d) To me, family means love, trust and security. It also means marrying and having children.
   e) I must admit that I sometimes dream of being wealthy, but it isn't a part of my future plans. There are other things which are more important than being wealthy, such as being healthy, having a good job and starting a family.
   f) Yes, I would say that lyrics and videos should be censored because there is often too much violence in videos and there are a lot of lyrics which create and encourage negative feelings.

V. Comment/Giving opinion

Hinweis: In dieser Aufgabe sollst du dich mit einem von dir gewählten Statement (Behauptung, Feststellung) auseinandersetzen. Formuliere deine Meinung, begründe diese und versuche, Beispiele aus deinem Erfahrungsbereich heranzuziehen. Achte darauf, deine schriftlichen Äußerungen logisch zu gliedern und auf die breits bekannten Wendungen zurückzugreifen.

- **Role models can have both a negative and a positive effect on youngsters.**
  I can fully agree with this statement. A lot of young people have role models, such as singers, actors or entertainers. Youngsters worship them because of their appearance or manner. They want to be like these stars, and dress and behave like them. But can such a superficial thing as a person's appearance have a positive influence on youngsters? I, personally, do not think so. To my mind, young people need a good example to be set by grown-ups in general. Family, friends, relatives or teachers can be role models who teach youngsters abilities and qualities which they need for their future. Learning from these people's experiences and learning strategies, methods and skills for life is important and has a positive effect on young people. To sum up, I would say that people around you can be good role models and can have a significant meaning for you.

- **Soaps and talk shows make you stupid.**
  Soaps and talkshows have become respectable because they are about the problems people have in life. They are regularly broadcast by TV networks and it is not hard to understand why millions of viewers not only follow them but also love watching them. But can soaps and talk shows make you stupid? I would say that depends on the individual, and so I can only partly agree with this statement. I can imagine that there are a lot of people – and especially young people – who cannot tell the difference between reality and the world shown in soaps and talk shows. So they are easily influenced. They can also often identify with the characters in soaps and the people in the daily talk shows because they are ordinary people like you and me. It is very likely that viewers see soap stars and talk show guests as role models, but I do not think that this can make you stupid. In conclusion, I think that although soaps and talk shows are not programmes of a standard high enough to widen people's horizons, the effect they have on people's intelligence is not necessarily negative.

- **Teaching behaviour at school has its pros and cons.**
  There is no doubt that behaviour is essential in all parts of life. And there are a lot of situations every day where we meet people who cannot behave. Therefore it is more necessary than we would like to admit that behaviour must be learned. But who should teach behaviour? To my mind, teaching behaviour is not the job of the school but of the parents. I must therefore disagree with the statement. I am convinced that parents are responsible for teaching behaviour. First, they should keep an eye on their children and be good role models. Furthermore, I think that teaching behaviour is strongly connected with upbringing. Children learn good manners in everyday family life because parents set standards. Certainly, school can help towards teaching manners in specific situations such as job interviews or examinations. However, I have come to the conclusion that family and parents have to do the job of teaching behaviour.

- **The values of the older generation are not ours.**
  I'm afraid I have to agree with this statement. To my mind, the differences between our generation and the older generation have grown increasingly over the last few years. There is a lot of disagreement and misunderstandings between the two. You often hear older people say that the young generation is lazy and disrespectful. And

we think that the older generation treats us like children. Therefore, both generations are prejudiced against each other. Although some of the older people's values and norms are accepted by the young people, we still have different moral values. Furthermore, our ideas of how to live often contrast sharply with theirs. However, this situation is against all reason. Therefore, I would say that older people should try to break down their prejudices against our way of living and we should behave more respectfully.

- **Wearing school uniforms is a good idea.**
Pupils in Britain are accustomed to wearing school uniform, whereas German pupils are allowed to wear what they like. This statement is very interesting, but I can only partly agree. As with all things, school uniform has its advantages and disadvantages. The advantages would be that young people would perhaps not attach as much importance to their clothes or to brand names, nobody would be bullied because of what they were wearing, as everybody would be wearing the same, it would make pupils identify with their school more, and in sports competitions between schools, uniforms would be a good way of recognizing the teams and their supporters. However, although there are a lot of arguments for wearing school uniform, I think clothes are a personal issue, and one which I would prefer to keep. As German schools often have strict rules about dress anyway, I think we should continue to be allowed to wear what we like.

- **Songs with bad language and a violent content shoul be censored.**
In my opinion, rock bands want to pass on information by means of their music and they want to create feelings. What message is passed on and what feelings are created depends on the intention of the band. I think there are too many bands which provoke violent and aggressive emotions, and therefore, I think songs with bad language and violent content should be censored. I fully agree with the statement.
It is a sad fact that there are a lot of songs containing lyrics which glorify violence. Youngsters listening to these lyrics constantly can easily be influenced. There are too many incidents every day which show that there is a connection between songs with bad language and violent content and aggressive behaviour. I suppose that censoring such songs cannot be the solution to the problem, but I am convinced that it could be a signal.
However, I think that most bands in the music business produce songs with acceptable lyrics, and that they intend to create emotions of joy and happiness.

- **You don't have to have talent to become a superstar.**
In view of the fact that such an untalented person as Daniel Küblböck became famous in the German superstar show, this statement would seem to be true. But fame is short-lived, and therefore I disagree with the statement. To my mind, being a superstar means being successful over a long period of time. There are so many singers, actors and actresses who became popular overnight with a song or a film, but who were then quickly forgotten. Therefore I think that real talent, fortune and good training are requirements for becoming and remaining a superstar. It is sad that many young people dream of becoming famous stars although they are not gifted. They take part in different casting shows and hope to be discovered.
But such dreams seldom come true in our fast-moving life. To sum up, I want to emphasize that we know from experience that only talent, opportunity and hard work make a superstar.

Ihre Meinung ist uns wichtig!

Ihre Anregungen sind uns immer willkommen. Bitte informieren Sie uns mit diesem Schein über Ihre Verbesserungsvorschläge!

Titel-Nr.	Seite	Vorschlag

Die echten Hilfen zum Lernen... **STARK**

14-V2N

Bitte ausfüllen und im frankierten Umschlag an uns einsenden. Für Fensterkuverts geeignet.

**STARK Verlag
Postfach 1852
85318 Freising**

Zutreffendes bitte ankreuzen!

Die Absenderin / der Absender ist:

- [ ] Lehrer/in in den Klassenstufen: _____
- [ ] Fachbetreuer/in
  Fächer: _____
- [ ] Seminarlehrer/in
  Fächer: _____
- [ ] Regierungsfachberater/in
  Fächer: _____
- [ ] Oberstufenbetreuer/in

- [ ] Schulleiter/in
- [ ] Referendar/in, Termin 2. Staatsexamen: _____
- [ ] Leiter/in Lehrerbibliothek
- [ ] Leiter/in Schülerbibliothek
- [ ] Sekretariat
- [ ] Eltern
- [ ] Schüler/in, Klasse: _____
- [ ] Sonstiges: _____

Unterrichtsfächer: (Bei Lehrkräften)

Kennen Sie Ihre Kundennummer?
Bitte hier eintragen.

Absender (Bitte in Druckbuchstaben!)

Name/Vorname

Straße/Nr.

PLZ/Ort

Telefon privat   Geburtsjahr

E-Mail-Adresse

Schule/Schulstempel (Bitte immer angeben!)

Sicher durch alle Klassen!

Faktenwissen und praxisgerechte Übungen mit vollständigen Lösungen.

Mathematik

Mathematik 5. Klasse Bayern .... Best.-Nr. 91410
Mathematik 8. Klasse Bayern .... Best.-Nr. 91406
Funktionen 8.–10. Klasse Bayern .... Best.-Nr. 91408
Formelsammlung Mathematik
Realschule 7.–10. Klasse .... Best.-Nr. 81400
Rechnen mit dem TI-83 Plus Sek. I .... Best.-Nr. 91409
Bayerischer Mathematiktest
9. Klasse – Realschule Bayern .... Best.-Nr. 91404
Lineare Gleichungssysteme .... Best.-Nr. 900122
Bruchzahlen und Dezimalbrüche .... Best.-Nr. 900061
Kompakt-Wissen Algebra .... Best.-Nr. 90016
Kompakt-Wissen Geometrie .... Best.-Nr. 90026
Entwicklung mathematischer Fähigkeiten
ab 4. Klasse, Teil 1: Algebra .... Best.-Nr. 990403
Entwicklung mathematischer Fähigkeiten
ab 4. Klasse, Teil 2: Geometrie .... Best.-Nr. 990405
Übertritt in weiterführende Schulen
4. Klasse .... Best.-Nr. 990404
Übertritt ins Gymnasium .... Best.-Nr. 90001

Betriebswirtschaftslehre/Rechnungswesen

Training 9. Klasse Bayern .... Best.-Nr. 91471
Training 9. Klasse Bayern – Lösungen .... Best.-Nr. 91471L
Training 10. Klasse Bayern .... Best.-Nr. 91472
Training 10. Klasse Bayern – Lösungen .... Best.-Nr. 91472L

Ratgeber für Schüler

Richtig Lernen
Tipps und Lernstrategien – Unterstufe .... Best.-Nr. 10481
Richtig Lernen
Tipps und Lernstrategien – Mittelstufe .... Best.-Nr. 10482

Französisch

Französisch – Sprechsituationen und
Dolmetschen mit 2 CDs .... Best.-Nr. 91461
Rechtschreibung und Diktat
1./2. Lernjahr mit 2 CDs .... Best.-Nr. 905501
Französisch – Wortschatzübung Mittelstufe .... Best.-Nr. 94510

Deutsch

Grammatik und Stil 5./6. Klasse .... Best.-Nr. 90406
Grammatik und Stil 7./8. Klasse .... Best.-Nr. 90407
Aufsatz 7./8. Klasse .... Best.-Nr. 91442
Aufsatz 9./10. Klasse
Realschule Baden-Württemberg .... Best.-Nr. 81440
Deutsch 9./10. Klasse
Journalistische Texte lesen, auswerten, schreiben Best.-Nr. 81442
Deutsche Rechtschreibung 5.–10. Klasse .... Best.-Nr. 90402
Kompakt-Wissen Deutsch
Rechtschreibung .... Best.-Nr. 944065
Deutsch – Übertritt in
weiterführende Schulen mit CD .... Best.-Nr. 994402
Lexikon Deutsch
Kinder- und Jugendliteratur .... Best.-Nr. 93443

Englisch

Englisch 5. Klasse .... Best.-Nr. 90505
Englisch – Hörverstehen 5. Klasse mit CD ..... Best.-Nr. 90512
Englisch – Rechtschreibung und Diktat
5. Klasse mit 3 CDs .... Best.-Nr. 90531
Englisch – Leseverstehen 5. Klasse .... Best.-Nr. 90526
Englisch – Wortschatzübung 5. Klasse mit CD .. Best.-Nr. 90518
Englisch 6. Klasse .... Best.-Nr. 90506
Englisch – Hörverstehen 6. Klasse mit CD ..... Best.-Nr. 90511
Englisch – Rechtschreibung und Diktat
6. Klasse mit CD .... Best.-Nr. 90532
Englisch – Leseverstehen 6. Klasse .... Best.-Nr. 90525
Englisch – Wortschatzübung 6. Klasse mit CD .. Best.-Nr. 90519
Englisch 7. Klasse .... Best.-Nr. 90507
Englisch – Hörverstehen 7. Klasse mit CD ..... Best.-Nr. 90513
Englisch 8. Klasse .... Best.-Nr. 90508
Englisch – Leseverstehen 8. Klasse .... Best.-Nr. 90522
Comprehension 1 / 8. Klasse .... Best.-Nr. 91453
Englisch 9. Klasse .... Best.-Nr. 90509
Englisch – Hörverstehen 9. Klasse mit CD ..... Best.-Nr. 90515
Englische Rechtschreibung 9./10. Klasse ...... Best.-Nr. 80453
Translation Practice 1 / ab 9. Klasse .... Best.-Nr. 80451
Comprehension 2 / 9. Klasse .... Best.-Nr. 91452
Textproduktion 9./10. Klasse .... Best.-Nr. 90541
Englisch 10. Klasse .... Best.-Nr. 90510
Englisch – Hörverstehen 10. Klasse mit CD .... Best.-Nr. 91457
Englisch – Leseverstehen 10. Klasse .... Best.-Nr. 90521
Translation Practice 2 / ab 10. Klasse .... Best.-Nr. 80452
Comprehension 3 / 10. Klasse .... Best.-Nr. 91454
Systematische Vokabelsammlung .... Best.-Nr. 91455

(Bitte blättern Sie um)

Abschluss-Prüfungsaufgaben

Mit vielen Jahrgängen der zentral gestellten Prüfungsaufgaben für den Realschulabschluss in Sachsen, Sachsen-Anhalt, Thüringen, Mecklenburg-Vorpommern und Baden-Württemberg, einschl. des aktuellen Jahrgangs. Mit vollständigen, schülergerechten Lösungen.

Mathematik

Realschulabschluss Mathematik
Mittelschule Sachsen .... Best.-Nr. 141500

Realschulabschluss Mathematik
Sekundarschule Sachsen-Anhalt .... Best.-Nr. 151500

Realschulabschluss Mathematik
Regelschule Thüringen .... Best.-Nr. 161500

Abschlussprüfung Mathematik
Realschule Mecklenburg-Vorpommern .... Best.-Nr. 131500

Abschlussprüfung Mathematik
Realschule Baden-Württemberg .... Best.-Nr. 81500

Physik

Realschulabschluss Physik
Mittelschule Sachsen .... Best.-Nr. 141530

Biologie

Realschulabschluss Biologie
Mittelschule Sachsen .... Best.-Nr. 141570

Chemie

Realschulabschluss Chemie
Mittelschule Sachsen .... Best.-Nr. 141573

Geografie

Realschulabschluss Geografie
Mündliche Prüfung
Mittelschule Sachsen .... Best.-Nr. 141590

Deutsch

Realschulabschluss Deutsch
Mittelschule Sachsen .... Best.-Nr. 141540

Realschulabschluss Deutsch
Sekundarschule Sachsen-Anhalt .... Best.-Nr. 151540

Realschulabschluss Deutsch
Regelschule Thüringen .... Best.-Nr. 161540

Abschlussprüfung Deutsch
Realschule Mecklenburg-Vorpommern .... Best.-Nr. 131540

Abschlussprüfung Deutsch
Realschule Baden-Württemberg .... Best.-Nr. 81540

Englisch

Realschulabschluss Englisch
Mittelschule Sachsen .... Best.-Nr. 141550

Realschulabschluss Englisch
Mündliche Prüfung
Sekundarschule Sachsen-Anhalt mit CD .... Best.-Nr. 151550

Realschulabschluss Englisch
Regelschule Thüringen .... Best.-Nr. 161550

Abschlussprüfung Englisch
Realschule Mecklenburg-Vorpommern .... Best.-Nr. 131550

Abschlussprüfung Englisch
Realschule Baden-Württemberg .... Best.-Nr. 81550

Abschlussprüfung Englisch
Realschule Bayern mit CD .... Best.-Nr. 91552

Natürlich führen wir noch mehr Titel für alle Schularten. Wir informieren Sie gerne!

Telefon: 0 81 61/179-0   **Internet: www.stark-verlag.de**
Telefax: 0 81 61/179-51   **E-Mail: info@stark-verlag.de**

Bestellungen bitte direkt an:
STARK Verlagsgesellschaft mbH & Co. KG · Postfach 1852 · 85318 Freising

STARK